KT-487-769

is

SOCIOLOGY IN ACTION

INVESTIGATING THE MEDIA

PAUL TROWLER

EG08242

UNWIN HYMAN

EG08242

EALING TERTIARY COLLEGE EALING GREEN CENTRE LIBRARY

Related Titles by Unwin Hyman

A History of the Mass Media   O. Bennett
Myths of Oz   J. Fiske *et al*
Finding Out About Society   L. Williams
Boxed In: Women and Television   H. Baehr and G. Dyer (Pandora)

302.23

ACTON TECHNICAL COLLEGE LIBRARY

Published in 1988 by
Unwin Hyman Limited
15/17 Broadwick Street
LONDON W1V 1FP

© Paul Trowler, 1988

All rights reserved. No part of this publication may be reproduced, stored
in a retrieval system or transmitted in any form, or by any means,
electronic, mechanical, photocopying, recording or otherwise, without
the prior permission of Unwin Hyman Limited.

British Library Cataloguing in Publication Data
Trowler, Paul
   Investigating the media.—(Sociology in action).
   1. Mass media – Sociological perspectives
   I. Title   II. Series
   302.2'34

   ISBN 0–7135–2832–X

Cover by Oxford Illustrators
Designed by Bob Wright

Typeset by August Filmsetting, Haydock, St Helens
Printed in Great Britain by Oxford University Press, Oxford

Contents

Introduction

The Sociology in Action series aims to provide readers with an interesting and up-to-date account of the main themes in the areas covered. The series has been written primarily for students following the Sociology 'A' and 'AS'-level syllabus. However, it is also designed to be helpful to those entering for GCSE examinations in Sociology, as well as related disciplines. To this end, each book relates the issues specific to its subject area to the broader concerns of social science and the humanities. The philosophy underlying the series has been to encourage students to deepen their understanding of the subject by engaging in short exercises and larger-scale projects as they progress through the books. The authors have followed the student-centred approach which provided the impetus for the establishment of the GCSE syllabuses and such innovative courses as the AEB's 'A' level Communication Studies and new 'A' level in Sociology.

Investigating the Media provides both a factual account of the mass media in Britain and examines the issues which have been, and are, the subjects of hot debate, not only in the social sciences but within the media themselves and in society as a whole. These include the question of political and other forms of bias in the media, the influence of the media on behaviour and the portrayal of women and racial minorities in the press, on television and on film.

The book includes exercises and projects which, it is hoped, will be developed and modified according to the aims and needs of the students and the facilities available. The book was written primarily from a sociological perspective but with the 'A' level Communication Studies syllabus and the GCSE Media Studies syllabuses also in mind. Students following such courses will find the suggested exercises and projects included here useful in making final decisions about their assessed assignments.

Paul Trowler

1 · Developments in the Media

Enjoy a whole new world of television entertainment...

with a Rediffusion Satellite System

So sophisticated... yet so simple!
Rediffusion takes the lead again
with the new RSR50 System!

REDIFFUSION

The quality choice in Satellite Television Systems

The mass media may be defined as 'the methods and organisations used by specialist social groups to convey messages to large, socially mixed and widely dispersed audiences'.

☐ In order to decide whether something qualifies as part of the 'mass media' it is possible to construct a table in the following way. Along the top horizontal axis it should have the questions shown below (they are derived from the definition of the mass media just given). Along the left vertical axis should be the thing you wish to test. If you can place a tick in the box under each of the questions at the top, then that thing qualifies as part of the mass media. Two examples are completed for you. Others you could test include: printed T shirts, graffiti on walls, books, video films, teletext, video games, a television set, computer software, records, photocopier, printing press, a television programme.

Example	Method or organisa-tion	Specialised social group	Messages conveyed?	Large audience?	Socially mixed?	Widely dispersed
Cinema Film	√	√	√	√	√	
The BBC	√	√	√	√	√	√

☐ Either individually or in small groups, make a list of ten predictions about what the media will be like in twenty years' time. Each list can then be read to the group and a discussion generated on the various predictions made and the reasons for them. Examples of things that might be examined are:

the number and type of TV channels
the use of computers in the home
the nature of newspapers, type and number
the extent of cable and satellite TV penetration
the existence (or not) of cinema/radio etc and their nature, and so on.

Developments in the broadcasting media

Broadcasting in Britain is divided into two distinct types: public and commercial. Public broadcasting is performed by the BBC, an organisation whose Board of Governors is appointed by the Government but which is otherwise independent (at least in theory). It is non-commercial, deriving income from the licence fee. Commercial (or 'independent') broadcasting until recently consisted only of private companies under the general control of the Independent Broadcasting Authority (the IBA), though some illegal private broadcasting did take place outside this framework. Thanks to developments in satellite broadcasting, however, the scope of independent broadcasting in Britain has widened in recent years, as we shall see.

The history of British broadcasting is summarised in Table 1.1.

Table 1.1: Developments in broadcasting media in Britain

1922   First public broadcasting begins (by private companies).

1926   British Broadcasting Corporation set up. BBC Radio begins broadcasting 'The National Programme'. Later diversified into 'The Home Service' and 'The Light Programme'.

Output of BBC directed by Board of Governers nominated by Government. Broadcasting financed by licence fees.

1936   BBC TV starts broadcasting. World's first public TV service.

1946   'The Music Programme' added to BBC Radio.

1951   600,000 TV viewers in Britain.

1954   Independent Television Authority (ITA) set up by Television Act.

1955   First ITA programmes begin transmission.

1956   6 million TV viewers.

1967   Radios 1, 2, 3 & 4 replace old BBC radio channels. BBC local radio begins.

1972   Independent Broadcasting Authority (IBA) replaces ITA. Commercial radio permitted locally by Sound Broadcasting Act. ILR (Independent Local Radio) begins.

1981   Broadcasting Act permits setting up of Channel 4. BBC gets new Charter to last until 1996.

1982   Channel 4 starts broadcasting.

1984   BBC news (for radio & TV) split into BBC TV News and BBC Radio News and Current Affairs Division. Cable and Broadcasting Act provides for Cable Authority and Satellite Broadcasting Board to be set up.

1986   BSB awarded satellite franchise by IBA (see below).

Independent television and radio is regionalised to a much greater extent than is BBC broadcasting, though the number of BBC local radio stations has increased dramatically in recent years. While local BBC television stations merely slot into the national channel at particular times, the ITV and ILR stations are responsible for almost the complete range of programming. The companies which provide commercial TV and radio broadcasting are illustrated in the two maps below:

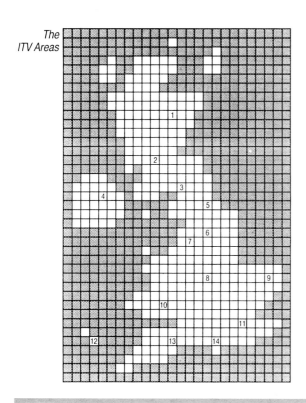

The ITV Areas

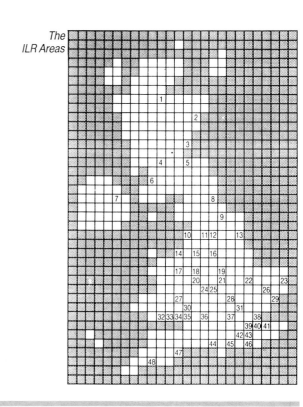

The ILR Areas

ITV AREAS
1 NORTH
   SCOTLAND
   Grampian
   Television
2 CENTRAL
   SCOTLAND
   Scottish Television
3 THE BORDERS
   Border Television
4 NORTHERN
   IRELAND
   Ulster Television
5 NORTH-EAST
   ENGLAND
   Tyne Tees
   Television
6 YORKSHIRE
   Yorkshire
   Television
7 NORTH-WEST
   ENGLAND
   Granada
   Television
8 EAST AND WEST
   MIDLANDS
   Central Television
9 EAST OF
   ENGLAND
   Anglia Television
10 WALES AND
   WEST OF
   ENGLAND
   HTV
11 LONDON
   Thames
   Television
   London Weekend
   Television
12 CHANNEL
   ISLANDS
   Channel
   Television
13 SOUTH-WEST
   ENGLAND
   TSW-Television
   South West
14 SOUTH AND
   SOUTH-EAST
   ENGLAND
   TVS

ILR AREAS
1 INVERNESS
   Moray Firth Radio
2 ABERDEEN
   Northsound Radio
3 DUNDEE/PERTH
   Radio Tay
4 GLASGOW
   Radio Clyde
5 EDINBURGH
   Radio Forth
6 AYR
   West Sound
7 BELFAST
   Downtown Radio
8 TYNE & WEAR
   Metro Radio
9 TEESSIDE
   Radio Tees
10 PRESTON &
   BLACKPOOL
   Red Rose Radio
11 BRADFORD/
   HUDDERSFIELD
   & HALIFAX
   Pennine Radio
12 LEEDS
   Radio Aire
13 HUMBERSIDE
   Viking Radio
14 LIVERPOOL
   Radio City
15 MANCHESTER
   Picadilly Radio

16 SHEFFIELD &
   ROTHERHAM/
   BARNSLEY/
   DONCASTER
   Radio Hallam
17 WREXHAM &
   DEESIDE
   Marcher Sound
18 STOKE-ON-
   TRENT
   Signal Radio
19 NOTTINGHAM
   Radio Trent
20 WOLVER-
   HAMPTON &
   BLACK
   COUNTRY
   Beacon Radio
21 LEICESTER
   Leicester Sound
22 PETER-
   BOROUGH
   Hereward Radio
23 GREAT
   YARMOUTH &
   NORWICH
   Radio Broadland
24 BIRMINGHAM
   BRMB
25 COVENTRY
   Mercia Sound
26 BURY ST.
   EDMUNDS
   Saxon Radio
27 HEREFORD/
   WORCESTER
   Radio Wyvern
28 NORTHAMPTON
   Hereward Radio
29 IPSWICH
   Radio Orwell
30 GLOUCESTER &
   CHELTENHAM
   Severn Sound
31 LUTON/
   BEDFORD
   Chiltern
   Radio
32 SWANSEA
   Swansea
   Sound
33 CARDIFF
   CBC
34 NEWPORT
   Gwent
   Broadcasting
35 BRISTOL
   Radio West
36 SWINDON/
   WEST WILTS.
   Wiltshire Radio
37 READING
   Radio 210
38 SOUTHEND/
   CHELMSFORD
   Essex Radio
39 LONDON
   LBC
40 LONDON
   Capital Radio
41 MAIDSTONE &
   MEDWAY/EAST
   KENT
   Invicta Radio
42 GUILDFORD
   County Sound
43 REIGATE &
   CRAWLEY
   Radio Mercury
44 BOURNEMOUTH
   Two Counties Radio
45 PORTSMOUTH
   Radio Victory
46 Southern Sound
47 EXETER/
   TORBAY
   Devon Air Radio
48 PLYMOUTH
   Plymouth Sound

The Government has traditionally kept a tight control over broadcasting through, for example, the appointment of the members of the BBC's Board of Governors and the IBA. Other elements of Government control include:

● the fact that while the private TV companies (Anglia, Central, LWT etc) do the actual broadcasting in commercial television their operation is monitored by a state-controlled body (the IBA)

● the government can amend the terms under which broadcasting bodies operate through changes in the law (Television and Broadcasting Acts) and in the BBC's Charter and/or Licence

● the government can deny the BBC an increase in the licence fee. It is effectively the BBC's paymaster.

Recently the ITV companies and the BBC have begun to lose their monopoly on broadcasting in Britain. This is largely due to increases in the number of homes with cable TV and the development of high power broadcasting satellites. While cable TV is not strictly 'broadcasting' (since the messages are not sent out over the air but via a cable—it is sometimes referred to as 'narrowcasting') cable stations are often fed their programmes by broadcasts from low-powered satellites.

Satellite television will probably prove to be the most important development in the media industry in recent years. Initially programmes could only be beamed to large dishes and then distributed to homes by means of a cable network. In 1985 there were 130,000 homes with cable TV. That meant about 500,000 viewers who could choose between a dozen channels, including the four broadcast channels. *Sky Channel*, one of the most famous of the satellite channels, reached 5 million homes in 1985, containing probably $12\frac{1}{2}$ million people. It is 80 per cent owned by Rupert Murdoch, owner of *The Times*, *The Sun*, *The News of the World*, amongst others, here and abroad (principally Australia). Cable television is different from broadcast television in that:

● it can be interactive (ie messages can be sent not only into the home but also out from it so that viewers can buy advertised products immediately, express preferences etc). Interactivity requires a particular type of cable network, called 'switched star' rather than the old fashioned 'tree and branch' cable network

● it offers more choice to viewers (in America there are over forty satellite-derived channels going into cable networks ranging from *MTV* (the music channel) to *Playboy Channel*. These now reach into $21\frac{1}{2}$ million American homes, an amazing figure considering that cabling started there only in 1976

● it offers the possibility of very localised channels—Milton Keynes has *Your Channel*, offering local news and information, on its cable network, for example

● it can have more freedom in terms of programming than broadcast TV, which is subject to lots of rules and regulations. *Premiere*, for example, showed *Emmanuelle 4* on Christmas Day 1985. It is doubtful whether it would be shown at all on BBC or commercial TV.

Recently the advent of high power broadcasting satellites whose messages can be picked up by small domestic dishes promises to transform this element of the media. Known as DBS (direct broadcasting by satellite), this technology removes the need for expensive cable laying, though at the same time it does mean that TV viewing cannot be interactive. DBS may offer an even greater range of programming than cable TV. What will DBS mean for the British viewer? There are essentially two opposing hypotheses; *'Unlimited Choice'* or *Wall-to-Wall Dallas'*.

The 'Unlimited Choice' hypothesis

DBS channels will compete for audiences by providing diversification in terms of content. They will become more specialised, appealing to groups in the population like the young, ethnic minorities, women and so on. This will ensure that they are popular among these groups and attractive to advertisers who know on which channel to advertise their products in order to make most sales. This especially will be the case with channels wholly or partly financed by advertising revenue. Subscription channels ('pay TV') may be broader in content. What sort of things could be available?

The No. 1 movie channel. Top movies and no commercials. Over 250 new films a year are shown on Premiere long before they are released on video or on BBC and ITV.

New round-the-clock entertainment channel for all the family, featuring popular BBC and ITV programmes plus sport, news and Musicbox all night pop music.

Offers a balanced range of programmes for children of all ages, with content and quality that parents can count on. They'll love it.

Cable Network News. A 24-hour continuous international news service, live from America. The first American channel for Europe.

- all-entertainment channels (soaps, situation comedy, music etc, like *Sky*)
- new film channels (*Premiere* and *Home Box Office*)
- international sport channels
- music for all tastes
- children's channels
- local news and events channels
- all-news channels with up-to-the-minute reporting
- programmes for ethnic minorities
- arts channels
- minority interest channels
- pornography channels (British law is powerless to stop foreign broadcasters).

This could lead to a future of almost unlimited (and unregulated) choice for the British viewer.

The 'Wall-to-Wall Dallas' Hypothesis

This argues that the content of DBS will be limited to soap operas, old American serials, quiz shows and spectacular shows, interspersed with pop videos. There won't be any serious drama, only limited news reporting, no documentaries and no analysis of business or politics. It will be the televisual equivalent of Radio 2—easy viewing rather than easy listening.

There are a number of reasons why this is so, according to this hypothesis:

● old American serials, pop videos etc cost the satellite company very little. To *buy* one episode of a serial costs between $3,000 and $7,000. To *make* it costs about $50,000 (1986 prices)

● undemanding programmes are popular with a large section of the audience. *Dallas* and *The Price is Right* have the twin virtues of being relatively cheap to buy or to make and they are guaranteed to pull in the audience (for the advertisers)

● buying American programmes has the advantage that their popularity rating has already been tested in that country

● because satellite channels transmit to countries across Europe the English language content of their programmes needs to be undemanding. *Sky Channel*, for example, has very large audiences in the Netherlands as well as in Britain. This makes difficult programmes about politics etc almost guaranteed to lose major parts of the audience

● unlike BBC and ITV there are no Government-imposed obligations on satellite channels to include a certain percentage of educational, political and other 'serious' programming into their schedules. Satellite companies are quite happy to leave this sort of material to the national broadcasting organisations of the various countries. The question is, though, how many people will continue to watch it if there are 'lighter' alternatives available?

The European sports network covering soccer, wrestling, speedway, ice hockey, baseball, tennis, golf, skating and lots more top international sporting action.

Top quality programming from the world of music, opera, drama and the visual arts.

Brings you a selection of programmes featuring all aspects of home and family life, including cooking, health and fitness, finance, advice, phone-ins and discussion shows.

One of the major national European TV channels, TV5 comes direct from France. Also available are RAI from Italy, SAT1 and 3SAT from Germany.

Which hypothesis is correct? The evidence from the USA and Europe, admittedly based on local broadcast and cable stations rather than DBS, seems to support the '*Wall-to-Wall Dallas*' option. Italy, for example, deregulated its television in 1976. This led to the creation of over 600 private channels. Their output consisted of everything from local community and news programmes to housewives taking their clothes off. At the early stage, then, there was much greater choice for the consumer. Soon, however, the small companies were swallowed up by Mondadore, a large TV company owned by Silvio Berlusconi. His station, *Channel 5*, thus gained a larger and larger audience. He soon set up a second channel, *Italia Uno*, then a third, *Rete 4*. Today Berlusconi's channels get 40 per cent of the TV audience while *RAI*, the state TV organisation which used to have a monopoly, also gets 40 per cent with the rest going to the remaining small channels. Now Berlusconi has moved to France and set up *La Cinque* (Channel 5). Small wonder that Berlusconi is known as 'His Transmittance' on the continent! Britain will come under Berlusconi's influence soon as he has teamed up with Robert Maxwell, the newspaper tycoon, to use the French DBS satellite TDF I to broadcast two channels to Britain and to the rest of Europe. This will carry advertisements and, one imagines, the same sort of content as Berlusconi's other channels. This consists of quiz shows, spectaculars, imported soaps, films, sport and, occasionally, science and nature programmes bought from abroad. Maxwell's current non-DBS channel, *Sky*, has much the same sort of thing. In America, too, the small cable channels are finding the financial going tough and are being swallowed by the big '*Wall-to-Wall Dallas*' companies.

In Britain the IBA has awarded (Dec 1986) the fifteen year franchise to broadcast satellite television to the British Satellite Broadcasting Consortium (BSB). This consists of Anglia and Granada TV, the Pearson Group, Amstrad and Virgin. Its income will come from a mixture of pay-as-you-view and advertising. It hopes, eventually, that half of British homes will have a £200 receiving dish enabling them to pick up the scrambled signal from the satellite. This will then be decoded by a black box on the TV set. Due to start broadcasting by 1990 at the earliest, programme content is planned to be:

- *NOW*—twenty-four hour news and current affairs
- *SCREEN*—feature films only (pay-as-you-view)
- *ZIG-ZAG*—children's channel (Walt Disney etc)
- *GALAXY*—entertainment channel (soap opera, quiz shows, drama etc).

It is still unclear whether the consortium will be successful in its plans. In the United States, where DBS has flopped due to the large number of cable channels available, the letters are said to stand for 'Don't Bother Starting'!

In all aspects of the media the consolidation and monopolisation of companies involved seems to be occurring, as happened in Italy. The British Relay Wireless Group was taken over by Electronic Rental Group in 1978 to make ERG the second largest rental group in the UK. ERG's controlling shareholder is the Dutch company Phillips Electronics. Phillips gave ERG a £10 million loan for the takeover. Phillips is the third largest company in the world in the field of consumer electronics after the American companies General Electric and ITT. Phillips owns Polygram and Phonogram and is a leading company in the research and development of new media technologies such as compact and video disc, video cassette recorders etc. Soon it may be in the position of being the manufacturer of most of the high technology media equipment sold in Britain and Europe, controlling the high street outlets which rent and sell this equipment and owning the major companies which produce the music and other software played on it. Such an extensive '*vertical integration*' (control over the supply of interdependent products) would give it a very powerful position in the media industry.

□ **What is your prediction about the future of DBS? Will it succeed in Britain or not? If it does will its content conform to the 'Wall-to-Wall Dallas' view or the 'Unlimited Choice' view?**

The press

In Britain the press is privately-owned. There are no Charters, licences or Press Acts through which Government attempts to maintain close control over the workings of the newspapers. Thus, the press is relatively free of Government interference, being a commercial enterprise rather than a public service. The main commercial aims of the press are to obtain as wide a circulation as possible and to achieve a healthy income from advertising revenue.

This is not to say, though, that there is *no* government control over the press. Such control can be brought to bear in a number of ways:

- the Official Secrets Act, section 2 of which prevents the passing on of information acquired through their job by anyone who holds, or has held, an office under the crown, held a contract made on behalf of the crown or worked under a person who holds or has held such an office or contract

- the Prevention of Terrorism Act has been used by the Government to prevent reporters writing about any contact with IRA and INLA. The Act was introduced in 1976 following a wave of IRA bombings in England. It proscribes membership of listed organisations with the aim of preventing a public display of support for them

- D notices are messages to editors of newspapers and those with editorial control in broadcasting. They advise such people that the Government considers a particular piece or category of information to be secret for the purposes of national security (D stands for defence). They ask the editor to refrain from publishing or broadcasting the information. These requests have no force of law and the Committee which issues them, the Defence, Press and Broadcasting Committee, consists not only of civil servants from relevant Government departments but representatives from the media industries themselves.

In addition to these government controls on the press there are others which may influence the content of newspapers.

- the law of libel means that journalists and editors in the mass media can be sued for saying anything which is defamatory about someone, ie something which damages the reputation of a person or tends to lower him/her in the eyes of ordinary men and women. This, however, is a law for the rich as cases are very expensive to bring

- the law of contempt prevents a newspaper publishing anything which is currently the subject of a court case ('*sub judice*'—under a judge) and which might prejudice that trial. This can be used to keep stories out of the press by keeping an issue *sub judice* for months or years through a series of court cases. Of course, this is an option only open to the rich, like multinational companies (eg Distillers, the makers of thalidomide) or the Government. A court injunction preventing the publication of Peter Wright's book *Spycatcher*, or any extracts from it, was used to suppress it in Britain while a court case in Australia brought by the British Government and lasting many months went on in 1986–7

- the Press Council is a body to which the public can complain about articles in the press (ie if they feel them to be untrue, unfair, immoral etc). However, this body has no real powers, other than giving bad publicity to newspapers they find to be at fault. Moreover, its deliberations are notoriously slow and its members are mainly recruited from the newspaper industry itself, a fact which casts doubt on its impartiality, to say the least

- the Advertising Standards Authority is independent of the advertising industry and has real teeth in the form of a code by which advertisers, agencies and the press have agreed to abide. A finding by the ASA against a particular advertisement in the press will result in its removal.

Recent developments in the press

The mid–1980s were important years in the newspaper industry. They saw the launching of several new national newspapers, *The Independent*, *Today*, *Sunday Sport* and *News on Sunday* being some of the most important additions. *The Independent* was launched by discontented journalists from other papers, led by Andreas Whittam-Smith, its current editor. It cost £18 million to launch (raised in the city) and has 210 staff. *Today*, originally the brainchild of Eddie Shah, was taken over by Lonrho and then Rupert Murdoch's News International. The editor now (1987) is David Montgomery and he targets it at 'go-getters': young, enterprising people spread right throughout the class structure. In the summer of 1987 it was losing £1 million a month. *Sunday Sport* is owned by David Sullivan, cost only £150,000 to launch and has an editorial staff of nine. Its editorial policy is 'tits, bums, QPR and roll your own fags': it has an average of fourteen pairs of nipples per edition. The target audience is males between sixteen and thirty-five years old.

Of these four new titles *Sunday Sport* is the only one making a profit. Its editor, Bill Nuttings, at one time had plans to make it a daily paper, though these have now been dropped. *News on Sunday* cost £6.5 million to launch and had thirty on its editorial staff after redundancies following receivership. It was saved by Owen Oysten/Growfair Ltd and the Transport and General Workers' Union. Oysten, an estate agency millionaire, saved the paper from bankruptcy, though it would clearly be a loss-maker for him. He wished to see a genuinely socialist Sunday newspaper. Its staff considered *Sunday Sport* to be 'junk journalism' and there was to be a competitive advertising campaign with the slogan:

NO TITS BUT A LOT OF BALLS

This was later dropped as being in bad taste.

Locally there were innumerable new titles, including *The London Daily News*, a competitor to *The London Standard*, launched by Robert Maxwell's Mirror Group, though this was later closed due to lack of adequate circulation. Many of these local newspapers are FDSs (Free Distribution Sheets). New printing technology has made possible the comparatively cheap and rapid printing of newspapers and permits a newspaper to be economically viable despite a fairly small circulation.

The diversity of these new publications, both in their content and political stance is perhaps best illustrated by comparing *News on Sunday* and *Sunday Sport*. The following was the editorial charter of *News on Sunday*:

NEWS ON SUNDAY
EDITORIAL CHARTER

News on Sunday's Editorial Charter has been drawn up by the paper's founders to set out the main editorial principles on which the paper is based. It is not intended to tie the editor's hands, but to set out in broad terms what the paper stands for and what it does not. A Founders' Trust has been set up with special rights to help ensure that the paper will continue to abide by the principles set out in the charter.

1. **NEWS ON SUNDAY** is a socialist publication. The open democratic nature of its socialism is spelt out in the principles outlined in the Charter.

2. **NEWS ON SUNDAY** is and will remain independent of all political parties and institutions. Its attitude to any political party will be guided by the extent to which its policies and practices accord with the general aims of *News on Sunday* as outlined in the Charter.

3. **NEWS ON SUNDAY** recognises that Britain is a society based on the unequal ownership of wealth, prosperity and power, and will seek to inform the readers of such inequalities, their causes and effects.

4. **NEWS ON SUNDAY** believes that everybody has the right to basic necessities—such as housing, education and health care—in the form of public services and a minimum income sufficient to maintain a decent standard of living.

5. **NEWS ON SUNDAY** is opposed to all forms of sexism, racism and all discrimination which denies the capabilities and potential of the individual.

    News on Sunday will express its commitment to anti-racism and anti-sexism both in its employment practices and in its news and feature coverage. It will reflect the multi-cultural composition of British society.

    As an employer *News on Sunday* is committed to providing genuine equality of opportunity. It will adopt the Equal Opportunities Statement from GLEB and will adhere to the Campaign for Press and Broadcasting Freedom's Code of Conduct on Sexism, the NUJ's guidelines on race and reporting on racist organisations, the NUJ's Equality Council guidelines on the coverage of homosexuality.

6. **NEWS ON SUNDAY** will support workers and their trade unions when they take industrial action, except in so far as action is in direct conflict with the principles in the Charter, and will seek to increase understanding of the origin and background of such conflicts.

7. **NEWS ON SUNDAY** will be internationalist in outlook. It will aim to increase understanding of all people and their cultures, particularly those striving for participatory democracy. The paper will support groups of people seeking to gain more control over their own lives. It will align itself with those whose beliefs are close to the beliefs expressed in the Charter.

News on Sunday will oppose the division of the world into power blocks.

News on Sunday will support the right to self-determination of all peoples. It will oppose interference by foreign states in the affairs of a country. The paper will support people fighting to free their country from foreign occupation, from racist regimes or from any form of dictatorship. *News on Sunday* will seek to increase understanding of the history and causes of such conflicts.

8. **NEWS ON SUNDAY** believes that the root cause of the present troubles in Ireland is the British presence in that country and the first step towards a solution can only be started once that presence is removed.

9. **NEWS ON SUNDAY** supports the civil liberties embodied in the NCCL Charter 1985. It will oppose moves towards increased police and military power and will support moves towards greater democratic control and accountability of state forces and freedom of information.

10. **NEWS ON SUNDAY** recognises the dangers of damaging the ecological balance of the world. The paper will advocate the conservation of natural resources, habitats and species and will support appropriate campaigns and movements.

11. **NEWS ON SUNDAY** opposes the imposition of suffering on animals in pursuit of profit or pleasure. Where such suffering is integral to medical research, *News on Sunday* will actively encourage alternative methods of research.

12. **NEWS ON SUNDAY** supports the demand for the worldwide abolition of nuclear, chemical and biological weapons. The paper believes that the unilateral abandonment by Britain of nuclear weapons, bases and alliances is a vital step towards this eventual goal.

On the day *News on Sunday* was launched, 26 April 1987, it led with a story about poverty in Latin America ('This Man's Kidney is For Sale'). Also, there was a warning that page eleven broke the Official Secrets Act (page eleven contained a menu from a Ministry of Defence canteen). Other stories included an article on the dangers of nuclear power, a page three picture of a punk Labour councillor (male), poverty and war in Mozambique (blaming South Africa), plus a colour supplement on archaeological finds in a South American desert.

On the same day *Sunday Sport*, set up in September 1986 by girlie magazine publisher David Sullivan, led with the story

ROYAL HOME SEX ORGY

This was about one girl and four men having an orgy for the benefit of a porn photographer in Lord Hertford's stately home. All but four and some of the sports pages had pictures of scantily-clad girls.

☐ **Examine the editorial charter of *News on Sunday* on pages 12–13, then attempt the following questions:**

1 **Do you believe that the low circulation and subsequent failure of *News on Sunday* resulted from the obviously political nature of its editorial policy?**

2 **What is your view of the idea that newspapers should have an explicit political stance like this?**

3 **Get a recent copy of any of the popular Sunday papers (*The News of the World, Sunday Sport*, etc). After close examination of its content, write a similar 'editorial charter' for that paper.**

Advertising is another striking difference. Adverts in *News on Sunday* were largely for jobs with Labour local authorities, those in *Sunday Sport* are for sex magazines ('showstopping naked starlets' etc), rude telephone messages ('Ring Emma to hear about Emma's Dream'), and giant posters of naked girls, including one with an allegedly 84 inch bust.

News on Sunday went into receivership in June 1987 after only a few months of operation, while the circulation of *Sunday Sport* reached a new high of over 500,000 sales (and a readership of over 1.5 million). *News on Sunday* finally closed in November 1987 after its circulation had dropped to 115,000 and even attempts by unions to ensure circulation by distributing it to members had failed.

Use of the new media in Britain

The new media include video casette recorders, computers and their software and other mass media based on high technology. It seems likely that children will be more willing to use the new mass media in the home than will their less-adaptable parents. Thus, if we are to assess how they will change our leisure habits in the future it seems sensible to study how children are using them at the moment.

On the basis of this reasoning a study was conducted for the IBA of 468 children between the ages of four and twelve years. The children were asked to answer a questionnaire and to fill in a diary logging their use of various media during a one-week period in 1986.

The results were as follows:

96 per cent had a computer at school
94 per cent had books at home
93 per cent had audio-cassettes
83 per cent had record players
65 per cent had their own radio
62 per cent had comics at home
52 per cent had a VCR at home (of whom 49 per cent said they used it regularly)
52 per cent had a computer at home (though only 20 per cent of these used it for purposes other than games)
43 per cent had 'their very own' television set
32 per cent claimed to read books fairly often
26 per cent claimed to read a newspaper fairly often
24 per cent claimed to read comics fairly often.

☐ **Compile a diagram to show the history of the press in Britain (use the one on page 6 about the history of broadcasting as a model). Sources of information to help you in this are marked with an asterisk in the bibliography at the end of this chapter.**

Some children, it was found, were 'media-rich' (ie, had access to an extensive range of mass media), while others (a smaller number) were 'media-poor'. Media-poor children had to make do with fewer sources of entertainment. The pattern of changing media use in the media-rich children was that the newer media displace the old only if they provide the same sort of gratifications that the old ones did but in a more attractive form—for example watching TV drama was found to replace the reading of comics (TV cartoons and drama are simply a more attractive form of comic). However, where *different* gratifications were involved then the new medium *supplemented* the old. For example, TV viewing in general did not appear to reduce the number of books, newspapers or magazines the children read.

☐ **The following tables relate to trends in some of the mass media. Study them and answer the questions which follow.**

Table 1.2: *TV-related equipment in the home in 1986*

% of viewers who have:	All adults	Adults with children
VCR	38	51
Home computer	18	33
Teletext	15	17
Video games	9	15
Cable TV	1	2
Video camera	1	1
Video-disc player	*	*
Prestel/Viewdata	*	*
have one or more of the above	50	68
have none of the above	50	32

(*less than 0.5%)

Source: *IBA Yearbook*, 1987, pp. 168–9

Table 1.3: *Viewing of bought/hired pre-recorded video cassettes in 1986*

% of VCR users who watch:	All adults	*Adults aged* 16–24	25–34	35–44	45–54	55–64	65+
Less than once a month	46	21	44	52	52	76	85
Once or more a month	26	32	28	27	22	14	—
Once or more a week	28	47	28	21	26	10	15

Source: *IBA Yearbook*, 1987

Table 1.4: *Current circulation figures of national newspapers*

	April–Sept. 1987	April–Sept. 1986	% change (—)
The Sun	4,021,122	4,035,117	(0.3)
The Daily Mirror	3,130,734	3,114,453	0.5
The Star	1,239,699	1,331,301	(6.9)
The Daily Mail	1,794,458	1,777,147	0.1
The Daily Express........................	1,675,070	1,773,708	(5.6)
Today	326,281	—	—
The Daily Telegraph	1,171,291	1,136,029	3.1
The Guardian	472,648	522,947	(9.6)
The Times.................................	446,790	478,404	(6.6)
The Independent	325,830	—	—
The Financial Times	299,036	253,180	18.1
The News of the World	5,021,366	4,881,644	2.9
The Sunday Mirror	3,001,732	3,012,586	(0.4)
The Sunday People	2,905,273	2,989,535	(2.8)
The Sunday Express....................	2,222,031	2,236,070	(0.6)
The Mail on Sunday	1,772,381	1,591,112	11.4
The Sunday Times.......................	1,234,398	1,126,730	9.6
The Observer	772,532	765,579	0.9
The Sunday Telegraph	732,808	675,937	8.4

Source: ABC.

☐ **What are the most significant trends shown by this table?**

What variables other than the presence or absence of children in the household may be associated with media use?

☐ **These IBA figures tell us about media use in Britain. The IBA consider that the variables of *age* and the presence or absence of *children* are the important ones. Hence, these appear in the tables. What other variables might be associated with media use?**

☐ **Current circulation figures can be found in the reference texts listed in the bibliography. Use them to establish which parts of the press are winning and which losing in the battle for increased circulation.**

Table 1.6: *Reading of national newspapers: by sex and social class, 1985*

	Percentage of adults reading each paper in 1985		Percentage of adults in each social class reading each paper in 1985						Readership (millions)		Readers per copy (numbers)
	Males	Females	A	B	C1	C2	D	E	1971	1985	1985
Daily newspapers											
The Sun	30	23	4	10	20	35	38	26	8.5	11.7	2.9
The Daily Mirror	24	18	5	10	17	27	30	18	13.8	9.3	3.0
The Daily Express	12	10	12	13	15	11	9	6	9.7	5.0	2.6
The Daily Mail	12	10	14	16	15	10	7	5	4.8	4.9	2.7
The Daily Star	12	8	2	2	6	13	16	10		4.2	2.9
The Daily Telegraph	7	6	30	18	8	2	2	1	3.6	2.9	2.4
The Guardian	4	3	8	10	4	2	1	1	1.1	1.5	3.1
The Times	4	3	16	9	4	1	1	—	1.1	1.4	2.9
The Financial Times	3	1	8	4	2	—	—	—	0.7	0.7	4.1
Any daily newspaper	72	64	72	67	66	71	73	58		30.0	
Sunday newspapers											
The News of the World	32	27	7	12	23	37	42	31	15.8	13.0	2.7
The Sunday Mirror	24	21	7	12	20	28	31	19	13.5	10.0	3.2
The Sunday People	21	19	6	9	17	25	28	20	14.4	8.9	3.0
The Sunday Express	16	15	29	25	20	12	9	7	10.4	6.7	2.8
The Mail on Sunday	12	11	15	17	16	10	6	4		4.9	3.0
The Sunday Times	11	8	37	23	12	4	3	2	3.7	4.1	3.3
The Sunday Telegraph	6	5	21	13	7	3	2	1	2.1	2.4	3.5
The Observer	6	5	17	13	7	3	2	1	2.4	2.4	3.2
Any Sunday newspaper	78	73	81	76	76	77	78	65		33.4	

Source: Table 10.5 *Social Trends 1987.* p. 165.

☐ **Which newspapers are most class/sex-specific? What reasons might there be for this?**

Four new newspapers are omitted: *News on Sunday, Today, Sunday Sport* and *The Independent.* What would be your estimate of their readership profile?

Table 1.7: *Radio: average amount of listening[1] per week in Britain*

Hours and minutes per head per week

	BBC National Radio								BBC Local Radio		Independent Local Radio		Other		Total	
	1		2		3		4									
	Hrs	mins	Hrs	mins	Hrs	mins	Hrs	mins	Hrs	mins	Hrs	mins	Hrs	mins	Hrs	mins
1976	3	09	2	18	0	11	1	17[3]	0	35	1	14	0	05	8	49
1980	3	07	2	41	0	10	1	05	0	38	1	27	0	12[3]	9	20
1981	2	49	2	27	0	12	1	03	0	38	1	53	0	15[3]	9	17
1982	2	53	2	20	0	10	1	07	0	47	2	29	0	15[3]	10	01
1983	2	54	2	04	0	10	1	07	0	46	2	09	0	13[3]	9	23
1984	2	38	1	44	0	10	1	03	0	46	1	59	0	24[3]	8	44
1985	2	36	1	31	0	10	1	02	0	52	1	58	0	31[3]	8	40

[1] Population aged 5 or over in 1976–1981 and aged 4 or over in 1982–1985.
[2] Figures for 1981 onwards are not precisely comparable with those for earlier years owing to changes in the Daily Survey methods used. [3] Includes BBC National Regions.

☐ **What trends are revealed here? Attempt to explain them.**

Table 1.8: Television viewing: by age, and sex

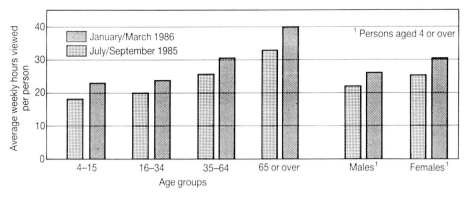

Source: Tables 10.2 and 10.3, *Social Trends 1987*, p. 164.

Table 1.9: Average weekly cinema admissions

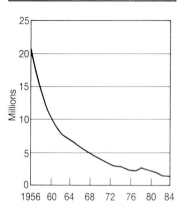

Source: Table 10.4 *Social Trends 1987*, p. 165.

☐ **Give four general statements we can make about TV viewing from these bar-charts.**

Try to give an explanation for each of them.

☐ **What explanations might there be for this trend?**

How could your hypotheses be tested?

Table 1.10: Use of VCR. Types of programme recorded (%)

	All with VCR	Age			Class		Sex		Adults with children
		16–34	35–55	55+	ABC1	C2DE	M	F	
Films	68	71	68	56	64	71	67	68	70
Soap Operas	46	56	40	34	44	48	34	56	51
Documentaries	27	18	35	32	29	25	29	25	25
Sports	22	18	25	24	20	24	29	16	20
Plays/drama	18	16	19	22	23	14	15	20	18
Adventure/police	9	10	7	10	9	9	11	8	10
Children's programmes	11	16	9	3	12	10	8	14	17
Comedy	8	8	9	6	10	7	10	6	8
Cartoons	5	8	4	1	5	6	5	6	8
Current affairs	2	1	4	3	3	2	4	1	2
News	2	1	3	1	1	2	2	1	2
Other types	16	10	8	13	10	9	10	10	10
'It depends'	2	3	4	8	4	4	6	3	3

Source: *IBA Attitudes to Broadcasting in 1986*, p. 23, Table 21.

Table 1.11: Viewing of bought/hired video cassettes in 1986 (%)

% of VCR users who watch:	All adults	16–24	25–34	Adults aged: 35–44	45–54	55–64	65+
less than once a month	46	21	44	52	52	76	85
once or more a month	26	32	28	27	22	14	—
once or more a week	28	47	28	21	26	10	15

Source: *IBA Yearbook 1987*, pp. 168–9.

☐ **What are the three most important pieces of information revealed by the above two tables about the use of VCRs in the home?**

Attempt to explain the three features you have identified.

☐ **PROJECT**

This project is designed to test whether being 'media-rich' or 'media-poor' affects the amount of time and attention devoted to school or college work at home among students. If you are studying in a school or college you may wish to use your colleagues for the experiment.

Firstly, design a questionnaire to establish whether, and to what extent, an individual is media-rich or media-poor (see page 14 for a discussion of these terms) and how much time is devoted to media use.

Secondly, add to the questionnaire a series of questions about time spent outside school or college doing assignments, studying for courses and so on. (You may wish to use other methods in addition or instead in order to establish this—eg, diary-keeping, interviews etc). You also need to gather information about the subjects and levels being studied to ensure that like is being compared to like.

☐ **ESSAY**

Consider the view that the need to transmit propaganda has been the most important factor influencing the development of communication technology in this century.

Thirdly, select as large a sample as possible on which to conduct your experiment. When you have collected the information you require, collate it in such a way as to establish whether and to what extent media poverty or wealth is correlated to time spent on studies.

Fourthly, write an account of the deficiencies of your methodology, including a discussion of other explanations of your results and other factors which may influence the 'studiousness' of students. These may be unrelated or only indirectly related to being media-rich or media-poor.

Bibliography

The items in the bibliography sections following each chapter are listed in order of relevance to the text, not alphabetical order.

R. Moorfoot, *Television in the 80's*, BBC, 1983

J. Cayford, *The Computer Media*, Comedia, London, 1986

P. Sieghart, *Microchips with Everything*, Comedia, London, 1985

G. Hodgson, *Television's Future*, Macmillan, London, 1987

R. Collins, *et al* (eds), *Media Culture and Society: A Critical Reader*, Sage, London, 1986

P. Marks Greenfield, *Mind and Media*, Fontana, London, 1984

T. Hollins, *Beyond Broadcasting: Into the Cable Age*, British Film Institute, 1984

A. Burkitt, *Cable and Satellite TV* W. H. Allen, London, 1986

S.M. De Luca, *Television's Transformation: the next 25 years*, Tantivity Press, London, 1980

D. McQuail, *New Media Politics*, Sage, London, 1986

J. Howkins, *New Technologies, New Policies?*, BFI, London

B. Gunter and B. Greenberg, *Media-Wise*, Times Educational Supplement, 3 October 1986, p. 52. (This is the source of the information on the IBA study of children's media use)

P. Lewis and C. Pearlman, *Media and Power: From Marconi to Murdoch*, Camden Press, London, 1986

*B. Whitaker, *News Limited: Why You Can't Read All About It*, Comedia, London, 1981

Reference texts

* *Willings Press Guide*, British Media Publications, (annually)

* *Benn's Media Directory*, Benn's Business Information Services Ltd, (annually)

Television and Radio, The IBA Yearbook, published annually by the IBA, London

BBC Handbook, published annually by the BBC, London

Note: Asterisks next to texts are for guidance in completing the exercise on page 14

2 · *Methods of Studying the Media*

The methods available to the sociologist in studying the mass media, and indeed most other subjects, are summarised in the following table:

Table 2.1: Methods of studying mass media

More quantitative	More qualitative
Asking questions	
structured interviews	unstructured interviews
closed-ended questionnaires	open-ended questionnaires
	discussion groups
Observation	
non-participant observation (can be quantitative or qualitative)	participant observation
content analysis	semiology
Secondary data	
official statistics	diaries, letters, autobiographies
Experiments	
controlled experiments (in the laboratory)	uncontrolled experiments (in the field)

We will examine each of the four broad categories briefly, explore some of the problems associated with each and give examples of a study or studies to illustrate it.

Asking questions

Questionnaires

Questionnaires are lists of questions which do not require the presence of a researcher. Their main advantage is that they are cheap and easy to use for the researcher and so a large number of responses can be gained. This means that the results are more likely to be accurate. However, the absence of the researcher means that questions may be misunderstood, not answered seriously or not answered at all—a high 'non-response rate' means that results may not be valid, despite a large sample size. Closed-ended questionnaires require 'tick the box'-type answers. Open-ended questionnaires leave the respondent free to answer as he/she wishes. Structured and unstructured *interviews* correspond to these two sorts of questionnaire, but they require the presence of a researcher to administer the questions and record the replies.

Both interviews and questionnaires are quite useful techniques for assessing people's attitudes towards the mass media, or, occasionally, gaining information about the specialist groups involved in the media; editors, producers etc. A form of very open-ended questionnaire was

☐ One advantage of such an open-ended question is that the researcher does not restrict answers in any way. Too tight a questionnaire may omit to explore issues which are important to the respondent but which the researcher has not thought to ask about. What other advantages and disadvantages are there to Ang's technique? Why not try a similar advertisement in your local paper, school or college magazine and see what results you get?

used by a Dutch sociologist, I. Ang, to assess people's attitudes to *Dallas*. This author put an advert in a Dutch women's magazine called *Viva*. It read:

> *I like watching the TV serial* Dallas, *but often get odd reactions to it. Would anyone like to write and tell me why you like watching it too, or dislike it? I should like to assimilate these reactions in my university thesis. Please write to...*

There were forty-two replies, 69 per cent of which were from women. These form the empirical basis of the research. The book consists largely of extracts from these letters and Ang's commentary on the reasons why *Dallas* is so fascinating a programme for viewers all over the world.

Interviews

Interviews can be structured or unstructured; that is, an administered questionnaire or an informal chat, or indeed a combination of these. In either case the presence of the researcher makes it possible to clarify and follow up questions, to check that answers are being given seriously and to ensure that the non-response rate is low. Problems with interviews include the fact that there will be smaller (and, therefore, less representative) samples than with questionnaires, there may be interviewer bias (ie, the interviewer may in some way affect the answers given) and simply the fact that people may say one thing but do, or think, another.

Unstructured interviews are often designed to get in-depth understanding of the respondents' attitudes and ideas. Like open-ended questionnaires, though, their results are difficult to collate, that is, to compare and organise different responses into a summary. Such problems are not met with structured interviews, the results of which can easily be expressed in quantitative terms.

☐ **Give three examples each of issues concerning the media which would be most suitably studied using:**
  ● **structured**
  ● **unstructured**
  interviews. In each case explain the reasons for your choice. Here is an example for guidance:

> *Issue: preferred channel for watching evening news and reasons*
> *Method: structured interviews with a random sample of people*
> *Reason for choice of method: limited options available so no need for elaboration.*

Interviews were conducted by D. Meehan for her book *Ladies of the Evening: Women Characters on Prime-Time Television.* She interviewed fifteen television writers, primarily because these are the creators of the events and characters on the screen and, thus, the source of any sexist images there. Similar interviews were conducted by M. Ferguson with the editors of women's magazines for her book *Forever Feminine.* Interviews are very frequently used in combination with other methodoligical techniques in studies of the media.

An interesting methodological technique was employed by L. Taylor and R. Mullan for their book *Uninvited Guests: The Intimate Secrets of*

Television and Radio. This involved the use of discussion groups. These consisted of nine or ten people chosen on the basis of their age, sex, social class and interest in the topic to be discussed. They met in a private house, were given a drink and then led in a discussion by a 'moderator' who gradually introduced a series of open-ended questions, ('Is there any resemblance between your family and the Ewings?', 'If Grange Hill were a real school, where would you like it to be?' etc).

They also carried out a small survey drawing on Fleet Street files and extensive interviews with a 'soap' gossip columnist.

☐ **Prepare a list of questions about attitudes to be administered to a group of people in the same way as this study. Ask about particular programmes, characters and plots to find out how people feel about them. Ask about how realistic they feel the programmes to be, who they identify with, whether they feel they learn anything and so on. If possible arrange for such a discussion group to meet, appoint a moderator and record the subsequent discussion. What similarities and differences between people's attitudes emerge? Are there any differences between the male and female answers, for example?**

Observation

'Non-participant observation' involves simply observing events as an uninvolved researcher. This may be covert (ie, hidden or secret) observation, or overt (in which participants know you are there and what you are doing). *Participant observation* requires the researcher to be involved in the action him/her self. This has the advantage of giving the researcher greater empathy with, and understanding of, the people concerned than is possible with non-participant observation. However, it has the danger that the researcher may be *so* involved that he/she can no longer give an impartial account of events.

Meehan's study illustrates the use of non-participant observation as well as interviews. She was permitted to 'sit in' on writing sessions for one week by the producers of the *The Bob Newhart Show*. A similar opportunity was afforded to Grant Noble by the editors of *Blue Peter.* They discussed the production of the show with him, showed him scripts and allowed him to watch rehearsals. This gave him several insights into the programme; how the illusion of intimacy is created by the nature of the set, the objectives *Blue Peter* has and so on. Perhaps the most interesting finding was the fact that the presenters of the programme are chosen to represent members of the family; one is the elder brother (John Noakes in those days), one is the father—older and unflappable (Peter Purves at that time). Finally there is the older sister (Valerie Singleton). The personalities the presenters project are carefully considered, the aim being to make the viewers feel comfortable and 'at home' with them and the programme.

☐ **Watch a current episode of *Blue Peter*. Do the personalities of the presenters still fit in with this model? Which presenter fills which role?**

☐ **What advantages and difficulties can you identify with studies of the media which are based wholly or partly on personal experience?**

Examples of *'participant observation'* of the workings of the media often come from those who have been employed in the media in the past and have then begun an academic career, or who have decided to write about their experiences. These include S. Hood *On Television* (Hood was an editor of BBC news), and N. Jones, who used his experience as Industrial Correspondent for BBC radio to write *Strikes and the Media: Communication and Conflict.* Other examples include

A. Hetherington, former controller of BBC Scotland, now an academic, and John Whale, the former ITN and *The Sunday Times* journalist who wrote *The Politics of the Media.*

'*Semiology*' involves the 'reading' of media output ('text', as semiologists call it, whether printed or not) for the hidden messages it is thought to convey. Media texts consist of 'signs'; that is symbolic content which evoke connotations in our minds. Editors, journalists and others in the media have developed expertise in the use of these signs, so much so that they are often not consciously aware of how or why they are using them. Similarly we, the audience are unconscious of the connotations they evoke in our minds. The best way to demonstrate this is through an example. News shots of policing of picket lines or inner city riots are often taken from behind the lines of the police. Thus, the viewer is encouraged to identify with the policeman and to share his fear and anxiety. The viewer sees the massed ranks of the potentially, or actually, violent crowd, perhaps throwing stones and other missiles at his/her vantage point. The camera shows two or three policemen dragging an injured colleague away, and then pans back to the crowd. The connotations here are: professional, organised but beleaguered police force face the mindlessly ferocious enemy. This interpretation of events is put in the mind of the viewer without the need for commentary. The viewer is usually unaware that he/she has been subtly encouraged to empathise with the police.

Semiology can be applied to any medium; film, cartoons, the printed word and even photographs (a picture is worth a thousand words, as the cliché goes, because of the hidden messages it contains). Semiological studies usually distinguish between the '*denotive*' and the '*connotive*' meaning hidden or encoded in media messages. Denotive codes are sets of symbols which have clear links to that which they signify, being tightly connected to them in a way which is not culturally specific. Connotive codes are constructed above these. They are more open and tend to depend on culturally-specific sets of meaning. They can be interpreted in one of a number of ways, though always within limits.

Cigarettes provide a good example to illustrate the difference between these two concepts. We can recognise a picture of a packet of cigarettes for what it represents quite easily, without needing to see the cigarettes inside it or to have any further clues about what the sign (the picture) signifies (a packet of cigarettes). This is the denotive code. Connotive codes are more subtle and could be read in a number of ways. In our culture cigarettes, thanks to the power of advertising, have come to be associated with such concepts as masculinity, ruggedness and reliability. These connotations are encouraged by the regular practice among cigarette advertisers of picturing cigarettes and cigarette packets in the hands of cowboys on the prairie, uniformed officers (presumably airline captains) at the wheel of sports cars and through sponsorship of sports which are thought to require these qualities. Sometimes the required connotive codes are made explicit by advertising copy, though this is usually unnecessary. An example comes from a magazine advertisement. The uniformed sleeve of the helicopter pilot rests on the door of his sports car, the helicopter visible in the wing mirror. The copy runs 'ROTHMANS ... WHEN YOU KNOW WHAT YOU'RE DOING.' A sample semiological reading of a photograph and associated copy is given on page 80.

☐ **Imagine you are a trade unionist making a short film about striker-police clashes on the picket line. Describe the sort of film you would make, including examples of pictures you would be looking for when you came to edit the film, interviews you would conduct and the commentary you would make.**

There are numerous critics of semiology. For example, A. Hetherington in *News, Newspapers and Television* is critical of the semiological work of Fiske and Hartley:

> '*Fiske and Hartley, . . .in analysing an item about Northern Ireland in* News at Ten *in January 1976 say that the images of soldiers on patrol, sandbagged positions and armoured troop-carriers were all intended to trigger the "myth" of "our lads out there, professional, well equipped". Possibly, but it is far more likely that the reporter in London and the film editor simply took the best library film available to them to illustrate a government decision announced by the Prime Minister in the Commons to send extra troops to South Armagh after fifteen people (five Catholics, ten Protestants) had been murdered near the border in two days. What is more, for those of the audience already sceptical about the effectiveness of military operations in Northern Ireland or antagonistic to the use of British troops, those images would do nothing to diminish their scepticism or antagonism.*'

☐ **Show a similar cartoon, for example, Scooby Doo, to a child or children under the age of twelve. Allow them to see five minutes of the episode only. Ask them which characters are goodies and which baddies, which will win and which lose, how the programme will finish, and so on (you will need to prepare your questions carefully in advance). Assess by their answers how true it is that children have developed a sophisticated understanding of this genre of TV programme and the universe inhabited by the characters in it.**

A combination of semiology and interviewing was carried out by Bob Hodge and David Tripp in *Children and Television.* They asked an experienced researcher to interview forty-two children from six different Australian schools after showing them part of an episode of *Fangface,* a cartoon show. The aim was to determine how the children responded to the show and how far they were able to decode it. The findings were that children developed quite sophisticated skills of semiological analysis up to at least the age of twelve. There are rules of the cartoon world which children actively learn. For example, they distinguish between the 'goody-goodies' and the merely 'good', between 'main characters' and 'not-so-main' ones. They know which sort of characters can be expected to solve problems in this type of cartoon, who will drive cars, who will eventually win and so on, even though they had not seen all of the episode in question. The world of the cartoon extends into the real world. Some characters are middle class some working class. Obviously some are male and some female and so on. Thus the children are taking in ideological content, which they have learnt to 'read' from an apparently unrealistic cartoon. However, Hodge and Tripp say that the ideological content is not uniform and it doesn't all go in one direction. This makes the overall effect difficult to establish.

'*Content analysis*' is a method of observation by which the content of published or broadcast material is analysed in order to measure some aspect or aspects of its content. A simple example would be counting the number of male compared to female characters in a series of advertisements. This would quantitatively demonstrate the sexism of advertisements. A more sophisticated version would analyse the sorts of occupations which men and women were portrayed as having. Content analysis is one of the most popular methods of studying the media. Probably the most famous British example of its use is the series of studies by the Glasgow University Media Group (GMG). These include *Bad News, More Bad News, Really Bad News* and *War and Peace News.* Their technique is broadly similar in each case, though they switch their focus of attention in each book. For *Bad News* they recorded the news broadcasts on all channels between January and June 1975. They carefully timed each item, noting the number and types of items in each broadcast (crime, industrial relations etc). The method of presentation was also noted (studio or outside broadcast, newscaster to camera, interview, visual display etc). Details of the people who appeared on the news were also taken, so that the level of access to the news for different types of people could be assessed. A computer was used to analyse the data which was fed into it after the news content had been broken down into quantitative form, in the way just described. The aim was to provide an objective, statistical account of the output of the news to show in which directions it was biased. In *Bad News* they were interested in the coverage of industrial disputes; in *More Bad News* this remained the focus, this time with more case studies and broader discussion. In *Really Bad News* they concentrated on political coverage in the news, including news broadcasts in the early 80s. The more recent *War and Peace News* looks at a series of case studies involving conflict of all sorts, from the 1982 Falklands dispute to the Greenham Common women and how the news handled these.

☐ **Because they studied the media *message* and not the effect on the audience, the GMG have to *assume* that if the news is biased then the attitudes it projects will be accepted by the audience. This may not be the case. Surveys of the public have found that very few people could remember much about what had been on TV news even the night before. Try thinking back to last night's news and listing the items on it. How much can you recall? Try the same exercise on others (you could make a note of the items on tonight's news and ask the question tomorrow).**
Finally, do you think it is necessary to be able to remember consciously the news for it to have an effect on attitudes?

The GMG had the financial and other resources of Glasgow University to help them, as well as a team of researchers. D.M. Meehan was less fortunate in that she had to work alone. For *Ladies of the Evening* she chose thirty-three American serialised dramas from between 1950 and 1980. She videotaped televised episodes of these and, where necessary, used film archives. In each case two episodes of each serial were studied in depth. These two were randomly selected. Additional episodes were studied for further information. She made notes as she viewed, supplementing the notes with scripts where available. Her results are summarised on page 96.

One big problem with content analysis is that in trying to turn the qualitative into the quantitative the tone and flavour of the initial text is lost, because this is very difficult to quantify. An attempt to get around this problem was made by the National Council for Commonwealth Immigrants. The front pages of four London weeklies were examined between August 1966 and January 1967. Stories involving ethnic identification were classified as 'unfavourable' (there were seventy-two of these), 'favourable' (twenty) and 'neutral' (thirty-two).

☐ **Can you see any drawbacks to this attempted remedy to the problem?**

Secondary data

Secondary data is information which has been collected from another source rather than through one's own primary research. Clearly it is a term which covers a whole variety of types of data; from official statistics through to personal letters, from video recording of TV programmes to analyses of film scripts by other researchers. Secondary data has the advantage of being cheap, easily available, often covering large populations, and it can be used comparitively (eg by looking at different countries' statistics). Unfortunately, it is often out of date, inaccurate or biased in some way and frequently collected for purposes other than that desired by the researcher using it.

Peter Hennessy in *What the Papers Never Said* puts secondary data to good use in the analysis of omissions (and therefore bias) in the newspaper reporting of politics and the study of how the press is manipulated by Government. The *thirty year rule* states that confidential cabinet documents may be released (with some censorship in the interests of national security) after thirty years. Hennessy's technique was to study both the archive material released under this rule and the newspapers of thirty years ago in order to compare what was *actually* going on in Government with what the newspapers were *saying* about it. Many examples are cited in the book of manipulation and deception by various Governments. One involves the setting up of a cabinet committee, known as GEN 325, to examine the question of immigration to Britain after ministers had become concerned that Britain might 'attract here an undue proportion of the surplus population of the West Indies and other colonial territories'. The work of GEN 325 and the concern of the Government on this issue would have been very newsworthy, but there was absolute secrecy while the committee met and no one even knew of its existence until the records were released in 1982.

Meehan, in the book referred to above, also studied newspaper stories and magazine advertisements from the same period as the TV dramas she was analysing (1950–5, 1955–60 etc). Additionally she examined studies which had been conducted by sociologists, historians, and 'communicologists' to give her a greater understanding of social and historical trends at the time. She also read accounts of the experiences of working women. This provided a database with which to compare the actual events of the world at the time and the events portrayed on the television screen. She was able to identify differences between the two and explore the reasons for them.

A study of the media which mixed the use of official statistics with content analysis and questionnaires was conducted by Bob Roshier. He analysed the crime reporting of *The Mirror*, *The Express* and *The Telegraph* together with *The Newcastle Journal* and *The News of the World* for the month of September in the years 1967, 1955 and 1938. His finding was that they all consistently over-reported all crimes against the person, robbery, fraud, blackmail and drugs compared with the official statistics on these crimes. Very markedly over-reported was murder. *The News of the World* consistently over-reported sex crimes (about one-third of its total crime reporting, compared to 5 per cent for the other papers). Crime stories which were serious or whimsical or with sentimental or dramatic circumstances were particularly likely to be reported. How did all this affect public perceptions of crime? Apparently very little. Respondents were closer to the official statistics than to newspaper reports in their estimate of the *amounts* of different crimes and in most other respects it appeared that their perceptions were little influenced by their papers. The main exceptions were that:

The nature of criminal offences in England and Wales in 1985

Total notifiable offences recorded: 3,611,900

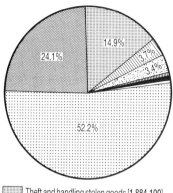

▦ Theft and handling stolen goods [1,884,100]
▧ Other[b] 0.3 [12,200]
▨ Sexual offences 0.6% [21,500]
▥ Robbery 0.7% [27,500]
■ Violence against the person [121,700]
□ Fraud and forgery [134,800]
▦ Criminal damage[a] [539,000]
▦ Burglary [871,100]

Source: Home Office *Statistical Bulletin, 4/86,* 13 March 1986; *Criminal Statistics for England and Wales 1985,* HMSO, November 1986

Notes:
(a) Includes offences of criminal damage valued at less than £20.
(b) Includes offences of 'trafficking in controlled drugs'.
(c) Bold figures in square brackets are the total numbers of offences recorded in each category.

☐ **What are the inadequacies in Roshier's study?**

- like the papers, respondents tended to over-estimate the amount of cleared-up crime
- *The News of the World* readers rated sex crimes as being particularly serious and particularly frequent. Whether this is a result of reading *The News of the World* or the reason they buy it in the first place is unclear.

☐ **Roshier's method was three-fold:**

- **a content analysis of newspapers to quantify the nature of their crime reporting**
- **a survey of those newspapers' readers on their views of crime, criminals etc**
- **an analysis of the official statistics for comparison.**

Try carrying out a similar project of your own. First, conduct a content analysis of crime reporting in one or more newspapers for a short period of time. Compare the results of this with the official statistics on types of crime, clear up rates, types of criminal and so on (these are available in *Social Trends* and in Home Office publications.) Then, construct a questionnaire about these issues. Conduct the survey and collate the results.

Experiments

'*Controlled experiments*' are so called because the researcher attempts to control all aspects of the experiment, all the variables involved, so that he/she can accurately establish cause and effect. In a natural science like biology this can be done fairly simply in the laboratory. For example, two identical plants are kept in identical conditions in the laboratory. Variables such as temperature, humidity, amount of sunlight, soil type etc, are carefully measured and kept constant for both plants. A single change is then introduced to only one of the plants, for example it is given more sunlight. The other plant, the 'control', remains as before. Any subsequent differences in the plants (size, speed of growth etc) should be the result of the differing amounts of sunlight they received as this was the only difference between them.

This method is excellent for establishing cause and effect. For this reason controlled experiments have been thought of as a good way of establishing the effects of the mass media on people's behaviour, particularly violent behaviour, and on their attitudes. Results can be checked, too, by replicating the experiment with other subjects to ensure that the effect discovered is a constant one.

'*Uncontrolled experiments*' are less rigorous. Here there is little or no attempt to control the variables involved or to measure the effects of the media in quantitative terms. Studies conducted in the field, rather than in the laboratory, come under this category. An example is a comparison of the behaviour of two groups of children, one with and the other without televisions. This sort of study is uncontrolled because there are numerous other factors which might affect behaviour other than the presence or absence of a television, but little or no attempt is made to take these into account.

An experimental study was conducted by C.R. Corder-Bolz involving

All in the Family, an American version of *Till Death Us Do Part,* with Archie Bunker as the American Alf Garnett. An episode was shown to children between the ages of five and eleven who watched in small groups and were interviewed about their attitudes to men's and women's roles both before and after it. This particular episode was about some neighbours of Bunker who had reversed the traditional sex roles. The result was that the sex role stereotyping decreased among the children after the programme, this effect being greater if an adult made such comments as 'look, the husband is doing the cooking, he seems to really like it' as the children watched. A similar study was conducted in Britain at the University of Kent on an episode of the children's programme *Rainbow.* This too had reversed sex roles and the results were the same. The variables are controlled here in the sense that there was no other influence on the children between the two sets of interviews other than the film they watched, therefore any change in their attitudes must be due to that.

There are a number of problems with this sort of approach:

- A film, viewed in a laboratory, perhaps alone or with a group of strangers, will almost certainly be different in its effects than one viewed at home with the family. The environment itself has an important influence on how one reacts to a stimulus, especially when the environment is as artificial as a university or other laboratory, with film cameras, one-way mirrors etc. The very fact that the subjects are being observed is highly likely to change their behaviour. This is a phenomenon sociologists refer to as the 'Hawthorne effect'

- Only short-term effects can be studied in a laboratory situation. It is unclear whether any influence remains or fades with time

- The groups chosen for study are usually unrepresentative, in terms of their social characteristics, of the population at large. Perhaps more important though, is the fact that no researcher has tried to isolate the different personality types and the different ways these may react to a media stimulus

- The nature of the experiments conducted are usually very artificial themselves. The films shown to subjects are often odd, isolated, violent episodes (adults dressed as cats hitting self-righting dolls with mallets etc). Then the subjects are put into a room after viewing with the same sort of items seen in the film. Even a young child is likely to get the message that it is expected to repeat the behaviour seen in the film

- Other people may mediate the influence of films and TV programmes. In the *two-step flow model* of the effect of the mass media it is suggested that other people influence how the media affect you through the comments they make about it and the discussions you have with other people about things you have seen, heard or read in the media

- The experimental method assumes that the *hypodermic model* of media effect is true. This sees the mass media as a hypodermic syringe which simply injects the audience with a message and they react to it through attitudinal or behavioural changes in the same way that the body does to, say, antibiotics.

This, of course, is far too simple. People watch, listen to and read the media for different reasons, with different amounts of attention and with different pre-existent attitudes. All these factors and others will affect how they, as individuals, are affected by a particular show. A more sophisticated perspective on media effects which *does* take this complexity into account is the *uses and gratifications* approach. It recognises that different people use the media in different ways and get different sorts of pleasure from them. For example, as attitudes solidify with age, changes such as those induced in the children discussed above are more difficult to bring about. Prejudiced adults will identify with, and find support for, their views in the Alf Garnett character of *Till Death Us Do Part* and *In Sickness and in Health*. Liberals will see the programme as exposing the ridiculousness of prejudiced thinking. For adults, then, such programmes reinforce existing attitudes, as the uses and gratifications approach suggests they would.

☐ **Imagine that you, either as an individual or as a group, have been given a grant of £20,000 (which must pay the salaries of the researchers and any costs) to conduct a study into the portrayal of alcohol and its consumption in television soap opera. The idea is to analyse what messages are conveyed about alcohol and what attitudes towards it might be created or reinforced among the audience. The body funding the research is interested in such details as who is seen drinking alcohol in soaps, why they do it, where and what the consequence of this consumption are. The relevance of alcohol to the plot and stories about the abuse of alcohol are of special interest.**

- **Which methods would you choose? (Consult the table at the beginning of the chapter.)**

- **Outline the details of the research—for example which programmes would you study, what sort of questions would you ask, what sort of people would you interview and how many, what will you look for?**

- **Justify the decisions you have made on these issues. If possible conduct the research.**

☐ **PROJECT**

This project is designed to test how far semiology is a viable method of studying media output. The aim is to determine how far the connotive codes of particular 'texts' are read in the same way by different people.

Select some people, preferably of mixed ages, social classes and of both sexes. Then select an example 'text' which you can use to explain the principles of semiology to them (a photograph like the one in the Johnson's advertisement on page 80 would probably be easiest). Explain the ideas behind semiology and give your reading of the example text. Then give a second text (again, possibly a photograph or an advertisement) to the individual and ask them to give their reading of it. This could be tape-recorded for later analysis and comparison with others. Repeat this process with the other people in your sample, using the same texts in each case. You could also ask people for their opinions of this method of studying the media.

☐ ESSAY

'The method chosen by the sociologist in studying the mass media will be influenced by both practical and theoretical considerations.' Discuss this statement, illustrating your answer with examples of studies of the mass media.

Critically assess any *two* studies of the mass media.

In your written report describe and give examples of semiology. Comment on how far the various readings of the same text which you obtained were similar and how far they diverged. Assess the implications of your findings for the validity of the method. Describe and discuss people's reactions to semiology as a method. Finally, give a general assessment of the method.

Bibliography

Bob Roshier, *The Selection of Crime News by the Press*, in Cohen and Young, *The Manufacture of News*, Constable, London, 1973, pp. 28–40

J. Fiske, *Introduction to Communication Studies*, Methuen, London, 1982

G. Noble, *Children in Front of the Small Screen*, Constable, London, 1975

J. Fiske and J. Hartley, *Reading TV*, Methuen, London, 1978

S. Hood, *On Television*, Pluto Press, London, 1983, (second edition)

J. Whale, *The Politics of the Media*, Fontana, London, 1977

D.M. Meehan, *Ladies of the Evening: Women Characters on Prime Time TV*, Scarecrow Press, NY, 1983

G. Tuchman, (ed), *Hearth and Home: Images of Women in the Mass Media*, Oxford University Press, New York, 1978

Bob Hodge and David Tripp, *Children and Television*, Blackwell, Oxford, 1986

A. Hetherington, *News, Newspapers and Television*, Macmillan, London 1985. (The quote in the text comes from page 17.)

M. De Camargo, *The Ideological Dimension of Media Messages*, Stencilled Occasional Paper, University of Birmingham, 1974

M. Ferguson, *Forever Feminine: Women's Magazines and the Cult of Femininity*, Heinemann, London, 1983

L. Taylor and R. Mullan, *Uninvited Guests: The Intimate Secrets of Television and Radio*, Chatto and Windus, London, 1986

I. Ang, *Watching Dallas*, Methuen and Co, NY, 1985

Peter Hennessy, *What the Papers Never Said*, Portcullis Press, London, 1985

J. Corner, *Codes and Cultural Analysis*, in R. Collins *et al*, *Media Culture and Society: A Critical Reader*, Sage Publications, London, 1986, pp.49–62

The Archie Bunker study is by C.R. Corder-Bolz, *Mediation: The Role of Significant Others*, Journal of Communication, 1980, 30, 106–18. The Rainbow study is from *Sex Roles and Children's Television*, Report to the IBA, Social Psychology Research Unit, University of Kent, Canterbury, 1983

N. McKeown, *Case Studies and Projects in Communication*, Methuen, London, 1982

M.G. Cantor and S. Pingree, *The Soap Opera*, Sage, London, 1983. (A review of different studies of that subject.)

J. Maynard, *Cable Television*, Collins, London, 1985

R.M. Negrine (ed), *Cable Television and the Future of Broadcasting*, Croom Helm, London, 1985

3 · Bias in the Media

This chapter asks whether the media are biased, and if so in what directions and why. The word 'bias' implies that something is one-sided or incomplete. Spotting it in the media is not simple. Though it is fairly easy to recognise prejudiced or loaded phrases and questions it is harder to identify *incompleteness* in a news report or a current affairs programme.

Studies of routine bias in the media have normally concentrated their attention on news stories. These cover important issues like politics and industrial relations where objectivity is important. This chapter will do the same, though others in the book examine bias in other types of media production (advertisements and comedies biased against women and blacks, for example).

The chapter examines three approaches to bias in the media; the manipulative, hegemonic and pluralist models. The manipulative model says that mass media manipulation is occurring in two senses:

- the content of the mass media is manipulated by those who own and control the institutions of broadcasting and the press, the men (and occasionally women) at the very top

- the hearts and minds of the audience are manipulated through this quite conscious control.

Thus, those at the top of the very small number of companies which own the media institutions use them for their own purposes. The media allow the rich and powerful to get richer and more powerful.

'Hegemony' means the dominance in society of one set of ideas. The hegemonic model says that the media in Britain help to recruit and maintain support for a single set of attitudes, ignoring others of equal validity. These, then, become seen by most people as 'normal' or 'just common sense'. Such opinions are not spread in a conscious and cynical way. They are simply what those who work in the media consider to be reasonable and true. This is because journalists, editors and so on come from a very small section of British society. They tend to be white, male, middle class and middle-aged. In other words they are a relatively privileged group. Because of this limited social standpoint the attitudes expressed through the mass media tend to involve (amongst other things):

approval of business and the creation of wealth
condemnation of excessive trade union powers or militancy
favour for consensus politics (ie pro-Liberal/SDP, middle-of-the-road
    policies)

support for the monarchy

suspicion of feminist women, black people, young people, the
    working class, radicals, gays, anti-nuclear protestors, strikers and
    so on

support for parliamentary democracy.

Generating people's approval for these ideas means that things go on much as they always have done. No voice is given to those who wish to change things in a radical way.

So far this sounds quite similar to the manipulative model. The differences between the two are as follows:

- the manipulative model argues that bosses control media content. The hegemonic model argues that journalists, editors, etc, do

- the manipulative model argues that bias in the media is consciously introduced. The hegemonic model says that the bias is unconscious (it stems from the attitudes of the people who work in the media)

- the manipulative model derives from a fairly rigid Marxist position which sees society as divided clearly between the capitalists (like Rupert Murdoch) and the proletariat. The hegemonic model sees society as broken up into an almost unlimited number of groups, each possessing a distinctive set of attitudes thanks to its social position (blacks, gays, women, the poor, etc).

The pluralist model simply says that while there *is* bias in the media this is perfectly acceptable because:

- the nature of the bias is determined by audience choice—that is, what the market wants and,

- there is a large number (a 'plurality') of media outlets, many of them adopting different types of bias for a different audience.

For example, it is quite clear that the popular newspapers over-report sex crimes relative to their proportion compared to other types of crime. However, there is no sinister reason for this. It is simply that this is what its readers want. Sections of the public who don't share that taste can turn to another newspaper (for example *The Times*). Bias, then, lies in the audience, not in the mass media.

The following table summarises the process of news production according to the three models:

Table 2.2: The process of news production according to the three models

Manipulative Model	Hegemonic Model	Pluralism
Hearing about the event Largely from and about *official* sources: parliament, the church, royalty, official "diary" events, local government, central government departments. Ordinary people are ignored for "serious" news. A limited number of capitalist press agencies supply (and virtually monopolise) a large amount of news. These include Reuters, Agence France Presse, United Press International and Associated Press.	**Hearing about the event** Largely from and about *official sources:* parliament, the church, royalty, official "diary" events, local government, central government departments. Ordinary people are ignored for "serious" news. Financial, technical and time limitations mean that stories are largely London based and from sources which are considered reliable and which have the resources to provide useful information quickly.	**Hearing about the event** Casual sources, "stringers", other media, aggrieved citizens, fire brigade, the courts, the police, the services, press conferences, press releases, companies, unions, pressure groups, local councils, the government, "diary" events, investigative reporting. In short a variety of sources which lead to a heterogeneous news content. Some sources are using the media to "axe-grind", but these are balanced by other axe-grinders of the opposite persuasion. The media present them all impartially.

Manipulative Model	Hegemonic Model	Pluralism

Assessing it for inclusion in the news

Manipulative Model:
A considerable amount of self-censorship occurs by journalists who have already been carefully chosen for their views. They will ignore or give a slanted angle of stories which will rock the boat too much (i.e. threaten those with power and influence). They will choose stories which fit the pattern of items on themes such as social security scroungers, "hippies" trying to organise rock festivals or anti-nuclear protests, football hooligans etc. Newspaper journalists ensure that the tone of the story fits the editorial policy of their newspaper. Proprietors and/or the government will interfere by adding or censoring stories where journalists are thought not to be doing this "properly".

Hegemonic Model:
It will be included if it is considered newsworthy. Newsworthiness is judged from the journalist's perspective; usually that of a white, middle class and London-based male (or at least what such a person judges other people to be interested in).

Pluralism:
Assessment of "newsworthiness"—this will depend on the nature of the medium:

POPULAR PRESS	POSH PRESS
scandalous	important
sexy	immediate
sensational	in depth
(particularly	
where personalities	
and conflict are	
involved)	

TV	RADIO
visual	non-visual
immediate	immediate
balanced	balanced

Preparing the story for the media

Manipulative Model:
In the press the story will be angled to fit the editorial policy of the newspaper. Important parts of the story may be left out if they represent a threat to the establishment (for example the reasons behind an industrial dispute, criticism of British political institutions etc.). In television the process of editing news film will result in a version which encourages the viewer to side with the forces of law and order, with the government and the establishment. Dissenting views will be characterised as coming from irrational people bent on destruction. Proprietors and/or the government will interfere in the editorial process if they feel that their interests or views are threatened.

Hegemonic Model:
The story will be interpreted according to the world view of the person writing the story/preparing the item. This view will be "encoded" in the language, camera shots, interviews, quotes, questions etc.

Pluralism:
The most interesting parts are selected and emphasised, these are the ones which are most relevant in some way to most of the pople (e.g. the *effects* of a strike rather than the events which led up to it—people are more interested in the former because it is likely to *affect them*).

Disseminating the message

Manipulative Model:
The institutions available to disseminate the message are few in number and either owned by capitalists or controlled by the government. Thus the means of dissemination are restricted to established media. Distribution of newspapers to newsagents is virtually a monopoly, with only three major wholesalers in the field (WH Smith, John Menzies and Surridge Dawson). In broadcasting, ITN and IRN service the news programmes of *all* the commercial television and radio programmes. Controls on the dissemination of information, such as the Official Secrets Act, D notices etc operate to protect the rich and the powerful.

Hegemonic Model:
The common background of journalists means that a similar message is transmitted no matter what the medium and despite the apparent variety of institutions in the press and publishing media. In order to appeal to the largest number of people the message is aimed at the lowest common denominator. Advertiser's demand that the interests of the affluent minority are catered for in a wide range of media aimed solely at them.

Pluralism:
Anything can be published unless it is obscene ("liable to deprave or corrupt") or seditious (anything that brings the Royal Family into hatred or contempt or excites disaffection against the sovereign or constitution) or libellous (a false and defamatory statement) or is in contravention of the Official Secrets Act. Anything which displays "due impartiality" and not obscene etc can be broadcast by the officially approved bodies.

Audience choice

Manipulative Model:
Despite the apparent wide variety of media outlets there is in fact little real audience choice. Channel 4 news and News at Ten are both ITN products, while BBC news differs only in trivial respects from either of them. Most large circulation newspapers are right wing.

Hegemonic Model:
There is no real audience choice. The same sort of people are involved in all the different types of mass media. As a result there is only one world view propagated through the mass media. This is usually the dominant ("hegemonic") one, though at times and in some media it may differ slightly from what those in positions of political power believe.

Pluralism:
Wide selection is available, particularly in the published media, but also in the broadcast media, especially since the advent of Channel 4, local radio stations (both independent and BBC), cable TV, satellite TV and video.

Effect on the audience

Manipulative Model:
With no scope for the expression of dissenting ideas in the media it is hardly surprising if the effect on the audience is to generate attitudes which are both uncritical and supportive of the status quo.

Hegemonic Model:
Alternative world views/experiences /attitudes are undermined. No expression is given for them, their value is denied. The hegemony of the dominant ideology is generally preserved and strengthened.

Pluralism:
Selective exposure (to the media)
Selective perception (of the message)
Selective retention (of the message)
the combined effect of these means that the media have little effect other than reinforcing previously held views.

News production: The manipulative model

'God made people read so that I could fill their brains with facts, facts, facts—and later tell them whom to love, whom to hate, and what to think.' (Lord Northcliffe.)

'I run the paper purely for the purpose of propaganda, and with no other motive.' (Lord Beaverbrook)

'Murdoch wanted to read proofs, write a leader if he felt like it, change the paper about and give instructions to the staff.' (S. Somerfield, editor of The News of the World *between 1960 and 1970)*

'On all the three continents where Mr Murdoch rules, his titles support businessmen, governments and their ambitions. It is an awesome power . . . which threatens our democracy. It is not simply because Mr Murdoch interferes with editorial policy, which he does, but because his staff from the moment they are employed know what is expected of them and they know what to write and how to write—and if they do not they will be out the front door before they can pick up their hat and coat.' (R. Corbett, MP for Birmingham Erdington, former journalist and NUJ national executive member, Hansard *6 July 1987.)*

The manipulative model states that the rich and powerful class who own or control the media use them to maintain the status quo. Radical ideas are suppressed, ridiculed or ignored. Attention is diverted from serious issues by a constant diet of trivia (television personalities, sexy stories and pictures, big-prize games, stories about the rich etc). The real foci of power are ignored and the attention of the audience is centred instead on institutions where power no longer resides (parliament, the monarchy, local government).

In many developing and socialist countries the media *are* consciously used for social engineering and control. In Britain, though, the press is privately owned and relatively unregulated by the state. Manipulation in this sector of the media is done by the 'press barons' like Rupert Murdoch. The broadcasting media, on the other hand, are indirectly controlled by the state. The state and capitalist interest, thus, work hand-in-hand.

Let's look at some of the evidence put forward by supporters of this theory to show that it is true.

● Ownership of the mass media is concentrated in a few companies. These also tend to own not just one type of medium but a variety (for example in publishing, broadcasting and cinemas). This is best demonstrated by the cases of Rupert Murdoch and Robert Maxwell.

☐ **Current patterns of ownership in the media can be identified easily by referring to Benn's *Media Directory* and Willing's *Press Guide* (see bibliography), and by writing to media companies for their current annual report. Their addresses can be found in the above directories. Use this information to establish a data-base, on a computer if you have access to one, on media ownership.**

Rupert Murdoch, Chairman of News International.

Owns *The Sun, Sun Day, The Times, The Sunday Times, Today, The Times Educational Supplement, The Times Higher Educational Supplement, The Times Literary Supplement, Times Books, The News of the World, Satellite TV PLC*, as well as other publishing, printing and paper manufacturing companies here and abroad. He controls one-third of daily newspaper sales in Britain, 35 per cent of British sundays and 60 per cent of Australian newspaper circulation. Additionally, Murdoch owns seven US local stations, *Sky Channel* (in Europe) and *20th Century Fox*. He is in partnership with the Belgian company Group Bruxelles Lambert, owns Metromedia (which makes *Dynasty*), and owns TV stations in Sydney and Melbourne. In Britain he is now moving into magazines. Murdoch Magazines (UK) already publishes *Elle* and *Sky Magazine* and its managing director, Elizabeth Rees-Jones, has plans to start many more. The first of these will be *New Woman* and *Automobile* both based on Murdoch-owned magazines in the US. In 1986 Murdoch acquired twenty-two American magazine titles.

Robert Maxwell, Chairman of the British Printing and Communication Company, Mirror Group Newspapers and Pergamon Press.

Owns *The Daily Mirror, The Sunday Mirror* and *The Sunday People* as well as less well-known publications as *The Scottish Daily Record, Sporting Life* and others. Mirror Group Newspapers control 21 per cent of daily newspaper sales in Britain in total. Maxwell also has holdings of 13 per cent in Central TV and 10 per cent of Mercia Sound. He owns Futura paperbacks and others, 40 per cent of Antelope productions (an independent production company), sole ownership of the country's largest network of local cable systems and a 20 per cent interest in the French high power DBS satellite TDF I through which he will broadcast programmes to Britain and Europe in conjunction with media magnate Berlusconi (see page 9).

- The fact that such companies as these have the power and desire to act together to stifle competition is shown by the fact that when the launch of the new paper *The Independent* was being prepared they tried a number of tactics to kill it at birth (this being the first new serious paper in 131 years). They offered its journalists 25 per cent more pay than *The Independent* would give (the journalists refused). *The Independent* was prevented from using some of the distribution services the others use. The other press companies tried to prevent *The Independent* from advertising on TV by trying to buy the space it wanted before it did (pushing the price of that space up from £35,000 to £51,000).

- The closeness to the political establishment of the 'press barons' is indicated by the very fact that they and those surrounding them very often *are* created barons, or at least knights, by prime ministers. This was true of Lord Rothermere (originally V. Harmsworth) of Associated Newspapers, Sir David English, editor of *The Daily Mail*, Lord Mathews of Express Newspapers, Sir Larry Lamb, editor of *The Daily Express*, Sir John Junor, editor of *The Sunday Express*, and, most recently, Lord Stevens, owner of United Newspapers.

- There is strong evidence that newspaper proprietors do attempt to control the content of the press. Such men as William Randolph Hearst (subject of the film *Citizen Kane*), Lord Beaverbrook, Lord Northcliffe and his brother Lord Rothermere and were quite open about their desire to manipulate the papers they owned and their ability to do so (lots of examples are given in *The Prerogative of the Harlot*—see Bibliography).

  Today's 'media barons' (their power now extends beyond the press) are in the same mould. They remove editors whose point of view they do not agree with (as Rupert Murdoch did with Harold Evans, editor of *The Times*, and Stafford Somerfield, editor of *The News of the World*). Mike Gabbert, editor of *The Star*, was sacked by Lord Stevens in 1987 for taking it too far down market. Its increasingly high nipple-count and its nickname of *The Daily Bonk* eventually became too much for Lord Stevens. He felt that its 'girlie magazine' image did not fit with his new status as a peer. Recently, Robert Maxwell, interviewing Magnus Linklater for the job of editor of *The London Daily News*, was in the middle of explaining that he did not interfere editorially when the editor of *The Daily Mirror* entered with a proof of page one from that paper for Maxwell's approval!

- The *distribution* as well as the production of the mass media is in the hands of the capitalist class. Newspaper wholesalers can (and do) refuse to handle radical papers. Their monopoly in many areas makes this an effective form of censorship. Three firms—W.H. Smith, John Menzies and Surridge Dawson—control 57 per cent of newspaper distribution in England and Wales. In Scotland Menzies alone controls 79 per cent of newspaper and 93 per cent of magazine distribution. In many towns they completely control the entire supply of newspapers and magazines. W.H. Smith has the monopoly in forty-three towns, Menzies in twenty-one, and Surridge Dawson in twenty. In September 1987, Rupert Murdoch's empire expanded further still through his acquisition of a one-third share of Martin's, the large national newsagent chain. Even the poster industry is now strongly monopolised. Just four contractors now own all 121,117 poster sites in Britain. As recently as 1986 the poster site contractors numbered around twenty.

- Evidence of *government* manipulation of the media is not difficult to find. Political correspondents know that Prime Ministers have consistently sought to use the media to strengthen their own position and to reinforce secrecy of government. It does this through informal pressure on those in control of editorial policy (for example, in the *Real Lives* case of 1985), through intervention in appointments, through the manipulation of political news content via the informal press briefings given by the PM's press secretary to lobby correspondents, and through the use of the Official Secrets Act where necessary.

The government can use its representatives on the 'D' notice committee to stop the publication of material it believes to be against the defence interests of the country, as happened when the chairman of the committee 'phoned the Reuters news agency and told them not to file a story about the position of the Canberra during the Falklands

□ **Use the 1985 edition of *Keesings Contemporary Archives* (found in most large libraries and the reference sections of college libraries) to research the background of the *Real Lives* affair. In the index look first under 'United Kingdom' and, under this heading, under 'Press and Other Media'.**

□ **Use the *British Humanities Index* for 1985 to find newspaper references to the case in which the government used the Official Secrets Act against Clive Ponting. Many large libraries have back copies of the broadsheet press, often on microfiche. Research the case using these once you have the references (which are filed in the BHI under Ponting's name in the index).**

dispute. However, informal pressure is usually the most effective (and secret). For example, Mrs Thatcher visited the Falkland Islands unexpectedly in January 1983. For security reasons it had not been announced in advance and as a result there was only one camera team there, a BBC one (despite loud hints which had been dropped by the Government to ITN). Wishing to make as much political capital out of the visit as possible, the PM's press secretary, Bernard Ingham, asked the BBC to share their film with ITN. The BBC refused. There then followed a radio-telephone conversation between Ingham and Alan Protheroe, the assistant director general of the BBC. Fortunately for us it was picked up by a radio ham in the Falklands. Mr Ingham said that there would be 'incalculable consequences' if the BBC did not share its film material with ITN. This seemed to be a direct threat of political repercussions for the BBC. Mr Ingham told Mr Protheroe, 'No film is coming out tonight unless I have your absolute assurance that it will be freely available to ITN and IRN'.

Eventually Mr Protheroe gave in and as a result TV and radio were full of long reports showing the Prime Minister windswept on the rugged island hillsides, joyfully receiving good wishes from Falklanders, and tearfully placing wreaths on the graves of fallen British soldiers. This did wonders for her political image.

The Government has the power of appointment of the BBC's Board of Governors and of the Independent Broadcasting Authority. Such appointments are made by 'the Queen in council', which in effect means the PM with the advice of the Home Secretary and occasionally the cabinet. The Board of Governors is surprisingly powerful; it appoints all the top BBC people, and has considerable powers of censorship, though the Director General and the Board of Management is in day-to-day control. Bill Morris, an official of the TGWU who served on the IBA's General Advisory Council, notes that there are 'plenty of middle class "high quality" appointees [to IBA bodies] but I look in vain for the dustman from Grimsby'. For example, the BBC's present Board of Governors (October '86) includes such representatives of the 'great and the good' as Lord Barnett (once chief secretary to the treasury—a government post), Sir John Boyd (an ex-right wing trade unionist) and Mr Malcolm McAlpine (of the famous construction firm). In October 1986, Marmaduke Hussey was appointed Chairman of the Board of Governors, an appointment described as 'outrageous and provocative' by the Labour Party due to his family ties with a cabinet minister, his connections with Ruper Murdoch's union-bashing at *The Times* and the commonly-held view that he was appointed to 'sort out' the BBC. Shortly after Hussey's appointment the Director General of the BBC, Alasdair Milne, was sacked. This followed a series of disputes with the government over such programmes as *Real Lives*, Panorama's *Maggie's Militant Tendency* and *Secret Society*, which had culminated in a police raid on BBC offices in Scotland to recover evidence for a possible prosecution of journalist Duncan Campbell and/or the BBC under the Official Secrets Act. Milne was replaced by Michael Checkland, known as an efficient but uncontroversial administrator. Informal control over appointments by the government also seems to operate. In 1985 it was discovered that MI5, the internal security service, vetted top appointments at the BBC, even placing newsreader Anna Ford under suspicion because of a previous boyfriend's political affiliations!

Control over the licence fee is another method through which the

Government can exercise pressure on the BBC. A. Hetherington, a former editor of *The Guardian* and Controller of BBC Scotland writes:

> '...discreet government pressure or informal persuasion is more likely to succeed [than direct pressure], and sensitivity to official attitudes must at times have influenced internal decisions. That has been particularly evident when the BBC's licence fee, its main source of revenue, is about to be settled. The mood of caution in the nine months before the 1977 settlement—never made explicit but amounting to "don't upset Downing Street"—was something that I experienced within the BBC at the time.'

News production: The hegemonic model

> 'The images on our television screens are the means ... of conveying an ideology: that view of society which has been evolved to provide a seemingly rational and therefore unquestionable explanation of how it works and of the power relationships within it.' (S. Hood, editor of BBC TV news 1958–61)

> '... the world view of journalists will pre-structure what is to be taken as important or significant ... it will affect the character and content of ... the news' (Glasgow University Media Group)

> '... news naturalises the (fairly narrow) terrain on which sectional ideologies can contend—it constantly maps the limits of controversy.' (J. Hartley, Understanding News)

The hegemonic model basically argues that the media portray only one view of the world (or *Weltanschauung*). It is the one subscribed to by society's privileged classes and it is the dominant, or hegemonic, set of ideas. The way we think and what appears to be common sense are pre-structured for us by the media so that they are in line with this Weltanschauung. Subordinate world views are allowed expression, but greater weight is given to the 'establishment' view. Indeed, allowing this apparent debate between, say, the views of the unions and those of management helps to build consensus in society. However, it is a consensus built around the dominant, hegemonic, ideology. Some views are rendered acceptable, normal or common sense. Others are seen as extremist, irrational, meaningless, utopian, or impractical.

Hegemonic theorists admit that the media in Britain are not, as a rule, directly commanded and organised by the state, neither do they directly speak for the ruling class. The reason for the bias in the media lies in the media professionals themselves. Media personnel are middle class, affluent people (usually men) who tend to take a 'reasonable', consensus-oriented view on most issues. Thus they will generally be pro-SDP, 'wet' Conservative and moderate Labour (ie, the middle ground of politics) and against extremism in any form. Because they are in the political centre, they have been attacked by both the left and the right, though most consistently by the left. This is because the media personnel will usually accept the establishment line on most issues. It is difficult to imagine someone like Sir Alisdair Burnett (at one time a contender for several Conservative constituency nominations) being able to sympathise with the point of view of black activists, Greenham Common peace protestors or striking miners.

The natural political inclinations of writers, journalists and editors are reinforced by secondary socialisation into the culture of the press and broadcasting media. They learn how strikes, for example, 'should' be treated (eg on TV it is considered best to use interesting film of the effects strikes have rather than boring talking heads discussing their causes). The content of virtually all the media reflects the perspective of the dominant group in society; white, male and middle class. Their hegemony is reinforced by media output—other, 'minority' views are seen as odd or peripheral. Sally Cline, once a journalist and woman's editor on a Fleet Street tabloid but now an ardent and active feminist admits that:

> *'I tried ... to be taken seriously. This meant I could not write about women or women's concerns ... I followed stereotypes of masculinity and femininity. If the women I interviewed broke the pattern, secretly I admired them and in print I lightly mocked them ... Each of my editors assured me that I wrote with what they termed "sparkle". This meant I was shallow, predictable and harmless ... Then, as now, I recognised that language can be used as a means of changing reality, but as a journalist I rarely tried to use it that way. On the occasions when I did, my copy would be spiked and my column would simply not appear ... I learnt to use it competently in order to belittle and betray blacks and homosexuals (these usually by omission), the working classes (these through stereotyping) and women (systematically through all available means).'*

Hegemonic theorists argue that those involved in the media unconsciously encode the dominant ideology when they create output for the media. This process involves selecting codes which put suitable meanings onto events and stories. The codes embody the 'natural' explanations which most members of their society would accept (that is, which appear naturally to embody the 'rationality' of a particular society). This process of encoding the dominant ideology, of giving weight to the views of the wealthy and powerful, is sometimes masked by professional values (news values, news sense, lively presentation, exciting pictures, good stories, hot news, good jokes). However these values themselves incorporate the dominant ideology. Decoding the messages in the media is a technique referred to as semiology. It is described in detail in chapter two and elsewhere in this book.

Let's briefly look at some of the evidence put forward by supporters of this theory to show that it is true. More detail on studies with this perspective can be found on pages 82–83 and 119–120.

- Evidence from careful studies shows that the media do set the agenda, set up a hierarchy of access etc. For example, in the pre World War Two economic depression the peaceful and non-political Jarrow Hunger March was given a great deal of publicity while less 'civic', more political marches such as those organised by the Unemployed Workmen's Association were ignored by the press and cinema newsreels at the time.

- Journalists are socialised into the culture of the institution for which they work. They quickly come to learn how stories should be presented and which are the important issues that should be

☐ **Buy all of today's tabloid newspapers (*The Sun, The Star,* etc). Choose a headline story on the front page of one of them. Identify the elements in it which make it 'newsworthy'. Classify all the stories in the papers into different categories and use these to identify the elements of newsworthiness in general which journalists and editors use. Identify the 'pattern' stories—ie one of a type which crop up regularly. Why does the type of story you have identified so regularly appear in the popular press?**

reported. When a new entrant to the IBA or BBC begins work he/she quickly learns to think about how their immediate superior will react to a particular story or approach. In case of doubt the policy is to always refer upwards, sometimes right up to the Director General. Newspapers have their own distinct culture too, though in this case also there are clear links with the dominant culture in society at large. In view of this it is not surprising that a past political editor of *The Sun*, Anthony Shrimsley, later became the Conservative Party's press and public relations officer.

☐ **Choose a news item from tonight's television news. Try re-writing the same story from a different perspective to that adopted by the editors and journalists of the news. For example, a story about Greenham Common could be re-written from the perspective of the peace women themselves, a story about inner city riots from the perspective of the people involved.**

● While there are a number of different news organisations even in broadcasting (IRN, ITN, BBC TV news and BBC radio news), the content of the news is remarkably similar. It is highly unlikely that this consensus about what constitutes 'news' and how it should be treated would exist if those involved in the media did not share a common world view.

☐ **Watch the news broadcasts at:**
  6.00 (BBC)
  7.00 (Channel 4)
  10.00 (ITV)
(This may be done only on one night or on successive nights, say for a week)

Make a careful note of:
1. **The type of stories they carry**
2. **The amount of time devoted to each story**
3. **How the story was covered (eg newsreader, interview, outside broadcast etc)**
4. **The overall 'tone' of the presentation (favourable, critical, neutral).**

Then, look for differences in the stories. Are the presentations basically similar, as the hegemonic model argues? Other possibilities for comparison are: *commercial vs BBC radio; different national BBC stations' news broadcasts,* etc.

News production: The pluralist model

'The Fleet Street newspapers of today offer the public a complete range of opinion and expression'. (Sir Max Aitken, Chairman of Beaverbrook Newspapers, 1966)

'The press is predominantly conservative in tone because its readers are. If any substantial number of people seriously wanted the structure of society rebuilt from the bottom, The Morning Star *would sell more copies than it does'. (John Whale, journalist and former ITN correspondent)*

'BBC and ITV enjoy a near monopoly, but they too must try to gauge the interest of their audiences if viewing figures are to be maintained.... The daily paper or news bulletin must be packaged or presented in ways that will attract attention and hold its audience. It must strike a responsible chord in the minds of viewers and readers'. (A. Hetherington, former controller of BBC Scotland)

'...The Sun *sells more copies a day than any other newspaper ... people enjoy the entertainment... it's won its place in the marketplace by providing the kind of material people wish to read ... if people wish to read it presumably they enjoy having their prejudices reciprocated'. (R. Greenslade former journalist on* The Sun, *speaking on* The Media Show, *27 May 1987.)*

The pluralist model agrees with the other two theories in saying that there is bias in particular elements of the media, inevitably so. However, taken as a whole the media cover almost all points of view. The audience need only select what they want to read, listen to or hear. The only consistent selectivity, other than bias which results from catering to audience tastes, is that imposed by technical constraints. These include the difficulties of reporting long-term processes, the problems of getting cameras to unpredictable events, the ease of covering London-based and predictable stories, lack of time and resources to cover stores properly and so on which all tend to shape the news in certain ways.

Let's look at some of the evidence put forward by supporters of this theory to show that it is true:

Another important finding which added weight to this outlook was that members of an audience differ greatly in the way they react to the same programme:

they reject it ...

they don't hear it ...

they switch it off ...

they ignore it ...

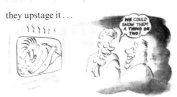

they upstage it ...

☐ **Give an example of three of the processes opposite from your own experience**

- The results of many empirical studies of the effect of the mass media suggest that rather than changing attitudes, the media serve to confirm those attitudes already held by the audience. The very earliest approaches to the study of media effects treated the message carried by the media as a 'Magic Bullet' or hypodermic syringe which, on contact with the audience, affected them in a uniform way. Later researchers realised, though, that things were not that simple. The audience was not really one undifferentiated mass, they were broken up into groups of people, each with their own pre-existent views. Moreover, the level of attention they devoted to the media and the motivations they had for using it were different. Thus was born the 'Uses and Gratifications' Approach to the media. This suggested that the following processes occur:
Selective exposure: The audience only tend to allow themselves to be exposed to messsages in the media with which they agree.
Selective perception: They react to media messages differently, depending on whether they strike a concordant or discordant note.
Selective retention: They are likely to retain in the memory only those messages which they consider valid or true.

Hence the tendency will generally be that the media confirm and reinforce existing views rather than having the power to change them.

- There is a large range of newspapers and magazines, radio and TV programmes available. Channel 4 in particular uses many small, independent producers of programmes and as a result offers a very varied output to its audience. Indeed, the Act of Parliament which set up Channel 4 requires it to be distinctively different from the others, catering for a whole range of needs and tastes. The choice available in the future will be even greater when DBS begins in earnest and cabling reaches even more homes. There are plenty of pro-Labour and Marxist magazines, too. The fact that people are not really interested in them is, however, demonstrated by their circulation figures: *The New Statesman* sells 29,500, while *The New Socialist* sells 13,000 and *Marxism Today* only 15,000 (mid-1987 figures). There is no difficulty in finding these magazines; they are sold at most newsagents, so there is no conspiracy to keep them off the news-stands. Furthermore, the Conservative governments of 1979–1988 have actively promoted deregulation of the media. As well as legislation promoting cable and satellite TV, in January 1988 they announced their intention to permit 3 new national commercial radio stations to be set up *outside* the control of the IBA, as well as provision for as many as several hundred new local and community radio stations. Douglas Hurd, the Home Secretary, said 'diversity underlies our whole approach to radio'.

Against the manipulative and hegemonic models, pluralist theorists argue that:

- While there is plenty of evidence to show that the ownership of the media is concentrated in the hands of a few capitalists, there is very limited evidence demonstrating that this actually affects the *content* of the media. In what ways does the magazine *Honey*, for example, further the interests of Reed International which publishes it (other than simply making profits for that company)? Indeed, theorists such as J. Burnham, A.A. Berle and G.C. Means strongly argue that managers, not owners, hold the real power. *Control* rather than *ownership* is the important factor in determining the output of the media. Thus editors and other managers determine the 'line' adopted by newspapers, films, magazines and TV programmes. This they do on marketing rather than political principles. Perhaps the supreme example of the media catering to public tastes is *Sunday Sport*. Set up in September 1986, it was deliberately intended to offer readers the 'best' bits of other papers, ie. what the audience enjoyed most. This was found to consist mainly of two things: sex and sport. Its proprietor, David Sullivan, makes no bones about this. News editor Rab Anderson says that he chooses stories by imagining what a twenty-five year-old bloke would want to look at before going to the pub. Indeed, 75 per cent of its readership are males between the ages of seventeen and forty-five and in classes C or D (see page 72). A typical lead story is about a part-time nun with an 84 inch bust. This approach seems to work, as its claimed sales by March 1987 were 493,000 with a readership of $1\frac{1}{2}$ million. This was before the launching of a Scottish edition and during the time when its advertising was banned by the IBA for being 'offensive'.

- Although *some* journalists and editors may feel that a certain amount of manipulation is going on from above, the vast majority

☐ **Compile a list of films, TV programmes, newspapers and magazines to illustrate the range of choice (in terms of political and other perspectives) available.**

☐ **Make a list of your interests/views which are not catered for in the mass media— these might be connected to your hobbies, the ethnic group you belong to, your age, your gender, or simply things you are interested in. Think about your friends and family too. Do the media cover the whole range of interests, and are those they omit left out for good reasons, do you think?**

do not. The quality and appeal of work are what determine whether or not it is included in media output. Journalists do not usually feel that any form of political censorship or manipulation is occurring. On the rare occasions when they do, they are willing to stand against it to maintain their professional integrity. This occurred in the *Real Lives* affair when TV journalists went on strike in support of editorial freedom. Editors and proprietors know very well that any attempt to interfere with the work of journalists will result in all kinds of problems. Usually it leads to their best staff going elsewhere. This is illustrated by an episode related in James Cameron's autobiography. He tells how he resigned from his job at the *Picture Post* over the censorship of an article he wrote during the Korean war. In it he criticised the brutality of the West's South Korean ally Synghman Rhee. The *Picture Post*'s proprietor Edward Hulton had demanded to have the article removed from the presses. Its editor Tom Hopkinson was fired for insisting that it be published. Cameron resigned but nonetheless went on to become a well-known and respected press and broadcasting journalist, despite his views.

● Many journalists, like James Cameron, are far from sharing the dominant ideology. A number of them are involved on a day-to-day basis with attempting to expose the unacceptable sides of capitalism. Even the Glasgow University Media Group have praise in this respect for investigative journalists like Jonathan Dimbleby. The Watergate scandal which saw the impeachment of US president Richard Nixon is just one example of the sort of work these reporters do. It was two newspaper journalists, Woodward and Bernstein (who worked for *The Washington Post*), smelling a 'scoop', who exposed the Nixon administration's misdeeds. In 1984, the report by *The Times* of Mrs Thatcher's banning of trade unions at GCHQ (the secret communications base at Cheltenham), showed the government in an unfavourable light.

Duncan Campbell's making of a film about a secret project for a spy satellite is another example. He argued that the government had misled parliament over this issue. While it is true that the government and Director-General of the BBC tried to stop the film being shown, it nonetheless got very wide coverage in the press and its contents were published in *The New Statesman* before it was eventually allowed to be shown on TV (in censored form).

● While some or most of the press are owned by relatively few companies, there are important sections of the published media which are independent of them. For example, *The Guardian* is owned by the Scott Trust set up after the paper's owner, C.P. Scott, died. The trustees take no profit: eight of them take no income or dividends whatever; only three draw a salary and rarely discuss editorial policy—usually at the request of the editor. Any profits are reinvested in the paper. Similarly *The Independent* claims to be free of proprietorial manipulation (hence the name), being controlled by those who work on it (including the editor). Those who work on the paper raised the finance to launch it themselves.

☐ **Buy a copy of the English translation of *Pravda* (now available at most large newsagents). Identify the differences between it and the British national press. Do these differences lend support to the idea of the 'freedom of the press' in Britain?**

● In countries where there undeniably is manipulation of the content of the mass media (eg. the Soviet Union), their subject-matter is quite different. News stories are almost exclusively about good news, not bad. Stories of crime and deviance do not appear. Stories critical of the powers-that-be or which put them in a bad light do not appear. This is the reverse of the British press.

● The fight between the TV companies for ever higher audience ratings and between the newspapers for higher circulations mean that both types of media have got to pander to popular tastes. They cannot afford to push a point of view on an unreceptive audience. Where vendettas are carried on by media proprietors, this is only to attract readers. Characters are chosen for vilification who are *already* unpopular with the public. Journalists have a keen sense of 'news values', that is, what the public will find interesting. These determine editorial content, nothing else.

☐ **The Royal Commission on the Press 1947–9 (The Ross Commission) asked newspapers proprietors, managers and journalists what constitutes news—ie what interested the British public. Their answer, in descending order of importance was:**

> **Sport**
> **News about people**
> **Strange or amusing adventures**
> **Tragedies, accidents**
> **Crime**
> **(last) Public affairs**

A. Hetherington provides us with the following list based on his experience as editor of *The Guardian*, 1956–75:

> *Significance*: social, economic, political, human
> *Drama*: the excitement, action and entertainment of the event
> *Surprise*: freshness, newness, and unpredictability
> *Personalities*: royal, political, 'showbiz', others
> *Sex*: scandal, crime, popular ingredients
> *Numbers*: the scale of the event, numbers of people affected
> *Proximity*: on our doorsteps, or 10,000 miles away.

Are your priorities the same? Rearrange these in your preferred order and add any that are missing. Also, try noting the items that appear on tonight's news and how long is given to them. Later, rearrange and re-time them according to your news values.

● Neither the manipulative nor the hegemonic model have much evidence to offer to show that the media do have an effect on the audience. Writers who support these approaches are usually theoretical rather than empirical in their approach. Even the Glasgow Media Group, whose work is based on empirical studies, do not study the effect on the audience of the messages they analyse. They are content to show that those messages are permeated with the dominant ideology. To be convincing, the hegemonic and manipulative theories need to demonstrate *an effect*. They have not done so.

● If the content of the media were really only propaganda or the embodiment of the dominant ideology, it would not appeal to people for whom it would be either boring or alien or both. In fact the mass media do appeal to the audience in their millions.

- Against the hegemonic model in particular, pluralists argue that the media cannot reflect the views of the dominant class in Britain because that class is itself highly critical of much of the political and other reporting of the broadcast media. Those on the right of the political spectrum argue that there is a 'liberal' bias in the BBC and some of the other media. In 1986 the Conservative Party's Chairman Norman Tebbitt complained bitterly about the BBC's reporting, by Kate Adie, of the American bombing raid on Libya. Other examples include a Panorama programme during the Falklands dispute (April 1982) which seemed anti-British, and another about right-wing infiltration into the Conservative Party (which was broadcast in January 1984 and called *Maggie's Militant Tendency*,) caused the government to become extremely angry. It resulted in a court case being brought by two Conservative MPs. This was settled out of court and an apology was made by the BBC. Another instance of 'liberal' bias in the media is the following: In September 1986, playwright Ian Curteis claimed he was asked by the BBC to make changes to his play about the Falklands because it shows Mrs Thatcher in too sympathetic a light.

☐ **In the right-wing journal *The Salisbury Review* (December 1987) there is an article by Curteis called *Bias and the BBC* (pp.10–13) which elaborates on these points. Use the library to get a copy of it. What is your response to the points he makes?**

The broadcast media, then, are accused of being pro right-wing by the left and pro left-wing by the right. One of them must be wrong, and the truth is that they probably *both* are. We have looked at the pluralist model's case against the other two views of the media, now let us examine:

The case against the pluralist model

- Far from increasing the range of opinions expressed in the media, the effect of market forces is to reduce them. This is at present apparent in the press and will become increasingly so as broadcasting is opened up to competition. The pressures of competition too often mean less space; fewer resources for journalists, especially correspondents; less scope for gathering background material on a story and increased reliance on a handful of newsagency sources. Also the tone of papers is likely to become very bland, designed to offend the fewest people and to cater to the lowest common denominator.

- The evidence suggests that the media *do* influence views, contrary to the pluralist's contention that the media merely reinforce views already held. Examples are given on pages 104–106 and 121–123.

- The ownership patterns of the media are highly monopolistic and are getting more so. So, even if the actual number of titles, channels, stations etc is increasing, the number of companies owning and controlling them is on the decline. In September 1987, for example, Rupert Murdoch gained a 13.5 per cent stake in Pearson, whose holdings include *The Financial Times* thus extending his empire further. This is leading to a decline in the range of views expressed. For example, many people believe that *The Times* has moved closer to the popular press since Murdoch took it over. Even the new satellite and cable TV channels are owned by the old companies or consortia of them (see page 34). In metropolitan areas there is usually a monopoly over local evening newspapers. In London the monopoly of *The Evening Standard* was only recently (February 1987) broken, and then only temporarily. It remains in other cities throughout the country.

- Journalists generally come from a very limited section of the population and hence articulate only a very limited view of the world. Applications for jobs are carefully sifted to exclude those who will not fit in. Even if not done deliberately, those doing the interviewing will tend to prefer those candidates who share their own background, views, manner of expression and so on. The same applies to promotion once the lucky candidate has got into the media institution. No-one is promoted unless they have acceptable views—which they will then put forward sincerely.

- Working-class newspapers close down despite large circulations because of lack of attractiveness to advertisers. The different ratios of advertising revenue are illustrated in the table on page 76: this shows how dependent the popular Sundays and dailies are on sales compared to other parts of the press. So despite having a larger readership, newspapers in this section of the market are fewer in number and less secure financially.

- The pluralist model is an inaccurate representation of news production in particular. Published news is monopolised by a few news agencies, predominantly AFP, UPI and Reuters. Broadcast news on all channels of radio and TV is totally controlled by only four institutions: IRN, ITN, BBC TV News and BBC Radio News. Thus the sources of news are not as diverse as the pluralist model would have us believe.

- The media do not respond to people's tastes, they create them. People may feel that the media are giving them what they want, but this is only because they have been 'trained' to enjoy that sort of product.

☐ **News items come from a variety of sources. Those identified in the table on page 32 include: casual sources, 'stringers', other media, aggrieved citizens, the fire brigade, the courts, the police, the services, press conferences, press releases, companies, unions, pressure groups with an interest in the publicity, local councils, the government, 'diary' events and investigative reporting.**

Watch or listen to tonight's broadcast news and try to identify what the likely source of each story was.

Item A: 'Dynasty', ABC Television (since 1980)

Blake Carrington, a self-made man, is an oil tycoon based in Denver, Colorado, and has a fortune estimated at $200 million. In 1954 he married Alexis Morell (Joan Collins) with whom he had three children, Adam, Fallon and Steven. Following her adultery in 1965, they were divorced. Alexis was given a generous financial settlement on condition that she did not visit the children. In 1980 Blake married his secretary, Krystle Jennings (Linda Evans). Accused of manslaughter, also in 1980, he was convicted largely on the testimony of Alexis.

Machinations by Blake's one-time friend, Cecil Colby, led in 1981 to Blake coming close to financial ruin and also to an explosion in which he temporarily lost his sight. In 1982 Alexis married Cecil Colby, who died immediately afterwards leaving her a controlling interest in his company, Colbyco, and instructions to destroy Blake. In the same year Krystle discovered her previous divorce was not valid, nor was her marriage to Blake. Alexis offered her a million dollars to leave Blake for good. However, in 1983 Krystle re-married Blake. In 1985 she had a daughter, Krystina Carrington.

Meanwhile, as chairman of Colbyco, Alexis has become the only woman to succeed in the oil business. In 1984 she persuaded Rashid Ahmed to double-cross Blake in a deal over South China oil, and in consequence Blake lost half his fortune. Alexis has since married Dex Dexter, and rediscovered her long-lost daughter, Amanda.

A. Easthope, *What A Man's Gotta Do*, Paladin, London 1986, p. 128.

Item B: 'EastEnders', BBC TV (since 1984). Audience: 20 million

The bi-weekly is an on-going serial about the life of a community in the East End of London. Being part of British history, the 'East End' location is instantly recognisable, and populated by a healthy mixture of multi-racial, larger-than-life 'characters'. It also has an inbuilt 'culture': a past ... the East End community—personified by the cockney—is lively, tough, proud and sharply funny. Our group of characters is fiercely territorial: incestuous almost—and reflects how life is TODAY in a very disadvantaged part of the inner city. Our area is the poorest borough in London, with the highest crime-rate, the highest unemployment and the largest collection of deprived minority groups—yet through all this apparent hardness, the dry, sharp and fast 'cockney' wit shines through ...

The specific location is a fairly run-down Victorian Square, part council-owned, and the regular characters are the inhabitants of that Square ...As well as one- and two-storey houses, the Square has a pub, a mini-supermarket, a launderette, a caff, and—under the railway bridge—the tail-end of a lively street market. 'Trendies' may soon creep into the area but for now it is basically working class with strong cockney culture and values ...

Families and family-life play a large part in the East End culture: families are frequently large, matriarchal and often with several generations living under the same roof. The bi-weekly theme is about relationships ... Who's doing what, to whom, and where, will be the constant gossip of the 'Square' ...[There are] different types of households and different generations of people, from babies to teenagers, to adults and grandparents. It's a small community that lives a fairly closed life and has many things in common. Elements of gossip, intrigue and scandal are high on the list of everyday happenings and events ...

J. Smith and T. Holland, *EastEnders—The Inside Story*, BBC Books, London 1987, p.19

Item C

Most academic critics, says D. Buckingham [author of Public Secrets—EastEnders and its Audience, *BFI Books], take the patronising view that TV promotes a single dominant value system which its audience simply absorbs. Not EastEnders. 'it contains a*

□ 1. **Using the evidence from Items A and B, what different representations of social class are being propagated in the soap operas referred to? (5 marks)**

2. **Describe and assess the ways researchers could study portrayals of class or status groups on television. (8 marks)**

3. **Bearing in mind the comments made in Item C, consider the role and impact of the soap operas with particular reference to their representations of class. (12 marks)**

range of different things, and invites a whole series of responses, rather than just one'. Each viewer gets something different—we all look into EastEnders for whatever approximates most closely to our own lives, and take comfort, instruction and enjoyment from that.

S. Summers, *The Serious Complexities of Life in Albert Square*, *The Independent* 16 December 1987.

☐ **PROJECT**

Construct an interview schedule concerning perceived bias in television news in comparison with other media. The following are some suggestions for the sorts of questions that you could include:

Do you think that **TV** news in general is biased (if so in what ways)?

Which is less biased: **BBC** news or **ITN** (including Channel 4)?

Do you trust your newspaper or television news more?

Which of the mass media do you gain most of your information about:

a) world news
b) national news
c) local news

Gather data also on the age, sex, social class and any other characteristics you consider important about your respondents.

Select a suitable sample of people and conduct the survey. Collate the results. Your task now is to establish whether there are any correlations between the perceived bias in the news and the characteristics of your respondents (their age, sex, social class etc).

☐ **ESSAY**

Examine the links that exist between ownership, control and production of the mass media. Refer to a range of media in your answer.

The press helps 'to advance public interest by publishing facts and opinions without which a democratic electorate cannot make responsible judgements.' (Royal Commission on the Press 1977) Explain and discuss.

Bibliography

S. Cline and D. Spender, *Reflecting Men (at twice their natural size)*, Andre Deutsch, London, 1987. The quote from Cline is on page 17.

Airwaves, The quarterly journal of the IBA Summer 1986. The quote from Bill Morris is on page 5.

P. Schlesinger, *Putting Reality Together*, Constable, London, 1978

P. Beharrell and G. Philo, *Trade Unions and the Media*, Macmillan, London, 1977

J. Curran and J. Seaton, *Power Without Responsibility*, Methuen, London, 1985

M. Cockerell, P. Hennessy and D. Walker, *Sources Close to the Prime Minister*, Macmillan, London, 1984

H. Cudlipp, *The Prerogative of the Harlot*, Bodley Head, London, 1980

CBI, *The Headline Business*, London, 1981

BFI, *Selling Pictures: The Companies You Keep*, London, 1983

S. Cohen, *et al*, *The Manufacture of the News*, Constable, London, 1973

A. Hetherington, *News, Newspapers and Television*, Macmillan, London, 1985 (Quote in text from page 30, the list at the end of the chapter comes from page 8.)

J. Burnham, *The Managerial Revolution*, Penguin, Harmondsworth, 1942

A.A. Berle and G.C. Means, *The Modern Corporation and Private Property*, 1968

Willings Press Guide, British Media Publications, (annually)

Benn's Media Directory, Benn's Business Information Services Ltd, (annually)

☐ **EastEnders: Mass culture, entertainment with a social conscience, or just entertainment?**

Mass media and mass culture

First we need to clarify our terms. 'Culture' is usually defined sociologically as that part of human action and its products which is learned through the process of socialisation (ie, it is passed on between the generations).

However, it has a second more common usage. In this sense it means the highest intellectual and artistic achievements of a society. Thus opera, art, literature and so on are considered to be 'culture' or 'high culture' and a person who is familiar with them is thought to be 'cultured'.

'Mass culture' is quite different. If 'culture' in the art and literature sense has very positive connotations, mass culture has very definite *negative* ones. It refers to art and thought which is artificial, produced deliberately for consumption by the masses rather than representing the highest achievements of dedicated effort.

☐ **In order to clarify the differences between these different meanings of culture (and, perhaps, show up some of the problems associated with them), construct a table based on the one below. Along the top horizontal axis are the different meanings of 'culture'. Along the left vertical axis are examples of social institutions and behaviour. Decide which category they each fall into. Two examples are completed for you. Others you could examine include: *Top of the Pops, Dallas, The Archers,* football, pop music, the English language, Mills and Boon novels, *Benny Hill,* the works of Shakespeare, sleeping, the sex drive. If you are working in a group or classroom situation, compare your completed tables. Make a note of the problems associated with the concept of 'mass culture' and 'high culture' that you encounter.**

Example	Part of:	Culture (sociological sense)	Culture (art and lit. sense)	Mass culture	None
The law		√			
Opera			√		

There are three theories which have dominated thinking about the influence of the mass media on culture, and in particular on mass culture. A shorthand way of referring to these is to call them 'the conservative right', 'the radical left', and 'pluralism'. Let us deal with their views in turn.

The conservative right

'Both TV channels now run weekly programmes in which popular records are played to teenagers and judged. While the music is performed, the cameras linger savagely over the faces of the audience. What a bottomless chasm of vacuity they reveal. Huge faces bloated with cheap confectionery and smeared with chain-store make-up, the open, sagging mouths and glazed eyes, the hands mindlessly drumming in time to the music, ... the shoddy, stereotyped ... clothes: here, apparently, is a collective portrait of a generation enslaved by a commercial machine.' (Paul Johnson, journalist, writing about the 'Menace of Beatleism' in 1964.)

This perspective on mass culture has dominated most thought about it. Its supporters include Neitzsche and T.S. Eliot, and many others in literature and journalism as well as some sociologists subscribe to it. Basically society is seen as divided between an elite (who possessed and still possess a superior kind of culture) and the mass of the population. In pre-industrial times the latter had a genuine, if somewhat rough, sort of culture of their own (perhaps 'folk culture' would be a good term to describe it). They could not appreciate Shakespeare or fine music, rich food or good wine. Nonetheless, folk culture had its particular qualities and character. It involved, for example, music, dancing styles (clog, morris etc), medical remedies and restoratives, recipes, folk tales, nursery rhymes, events like carnivals, festivals and so on. These were passed down in a more-or-less unchanging way between the generations. Their precise characteristics differed somewhat around the country. Workers were happy with their lot, with family life and with their cultural mileu.

However, capitalism quickly polluted that culture and replaced it with a plastic commodity culture—mass culture. Big business and the state began to replace the family as the source of culture. The old traditions were quickly wiped out in most parts of the country. The working man and woman have become passive recipients of culture, not active participants in it. Today they sit in the cinema rather than take part in the folk dance. They buy fast food rather than make good food themselves with traditional recipes. Advertising has given them the constant desire for things which they can't have. Their world is filled with characters from the television who they don't really know, though they spend hours reading and talking about them as they once might have done about characters in the village. The mass media are particularly implicated in this as it has been their role to transmit and propagate mass culture.

All this has made the working class listless and alienated. They are no longer content with their condition in life. Many of the problems of capitalism (strikes, violence, riots, suicides, divorce etc) are at least partly due to the inauthentic nature of the culture created for the masses by that economic system. All this is mainly the fault of the mass media. Their effect has been:

'a diffusion among the audience of a sense of apathy. The intense involvement of the masses with their culture at the turn of the century has given way to passive acquiescence'. (O. Handlin, 1964)

☐ **The quote at the beginning of this section comes from, and refers to, 1964. Write an updated paragraph as if you were Paul Johnson. (You might refer to current TV programmes, magazines for young people, pop music or any other aspect of the contemporary mass media.)**

The radical left

They're pointing out the enemy to keep you deaf and blind
They wanna sap your energy, incarcerate your mind
They give you Rule Brittania, gassy beer, page 3
Two weeks in Espana and Sunday Striptease.
                    (Dire Straits Industrial Disease, *1982)*

Those who formulated this perspective on mass culture in an academic way are usually collectively referred to as *The Frankfurt School.* They include such writers as T. Adorno, H. Marcuse and M. Horkheimer. Many of them were fugitives to America from Hitler's Germany. Most took up academic posts in America where the theory of mass society and mass culture was developed.

These writers, like the ones just discussed, are highly critical of capitalism, and for reasons which at first sight appear similar. They believe that the working class was once both dynamic and progressive. However, the capitalist system has made that class soul-less and one-dimensional. Traditional centres of authority, like the family, have been replaced by the state and by big business. These provide a schooling system, lifestyle and entertainments which make the working class passive, uncritical, unthinking. Believing they are free, people are really manipulated. Believing they are happy, people are really in a 'euphoria of unhappiness'. In a sense this theory is a more complex elaboration of the idea that the working class are pacified by 'bread and circuses'. The rulers believe of the working class that all they need do is keep their bellies full and their minds busy with entertainment and they won't give any trouble: 'The hypnotic power of the mass media deprive us of the capacity for critical thought which is essential if we are to change the world' (Marcuse).

The Frankfurt school sees the modern equivalent of bread as being all the consumer items that modern capitalism can provide. The circuses are the many elements which collectively comprise mass culture; page 3 girls, Royalty, TV stars, football, soap operas, and so on. Those in authority within capitalism are able to propagate a myth of freedom and of choice. The masses are kept happy. They do not recognise the repressive nature of their 'freedom'.

☐ **The Royal Family: Media favourites**

Add speech bubbles.

What is *your* view on the reasons for the great media interest in the Royal Family?

We can illustrate these ideas by looking at the concept of 'the permissive society'. It is usually said about the 1960s that they were years which marked the beginning of new freedoms. People could, for the first time, explore their sexuality and other previously repressed desires. Fashion and other styles were liberated from the constraints under which they had operated in the past. However, the concept of 'permissiveness' contains all sorts of internal contradictions. It implies that someone is allowing ('permitting') freedom. But, freedom is not really freedom if it is merely sanctioned by some higher authority, perhaps temporarily. For the Frankfurt school the sexual liberation of the '60s and later is an integral part of mass culture. Modern sexuality is not *real* sexuality, it is in a form which Marcuse refers to as 'repressive desublimation'. To sublimate something is to repress it. To de-sublimate it is, therefore, to give it expression. But repressive desublimation, an apparent contradiction in terms, means to give expression to, for example, sexuality, in a repressive way. An illustration would be the trivial sexiness and superficial eroticism expressed in the advertising world and in *Sunday Sport*.

The aim of all this repression disguised as liberation is to keep the people passive and feeling content. The working class are potentially a revolutionary force, capable of overthrowing capitalism. The way to stop them doing so is to give them material well-being and the illusion of freedom. The mass media, the welfare state and the consumer society are all crucial in this effort.

Here, then, is the important difference between the conservative right and the radical left. The first sees the natural state of the working class as contented and static. The second sees it as discontented and dynamic. The first sees capitalism as disrupting this natural state by causing unease and discontent. The second sees it as repressing the natural state by creating a sense of ease and well-being.

> The radical left argue that the main function of the media is to titillate and entertain, so that the attention and interests of the working class are diverted from serious issues such as their exploited position in modern capitalism. The extensive coverage of 'The Royals' does this particularly well. List other topics which appear regularly in the media (both printed and broadcast) which could be said to perform this function. What arguments could be used *against* the view that their purpose is to pacify the working class by keeping them 'happy'?

Pluralism

> '*A fairly uniform pattern of mass media use is now common to all social strata in industrial societies, and judgements of what is "good" and "bad" have become blurred ... it seems now possible to conclude that ... industrial society does have something like a common culture which is that provided by the entertainment media.*' (D. Bell, The Coming of Post-Industrial Society)

Academic supporters of this view include D. Bell and E. Shils. Many of those working in the media would also subscribe to it. Pluralists reject the view that there is a 'mass culture' at all, at least in the negative sense that that term is used by the other two perspectives. For the pluralists it is not true that the working class had a 'true' or pure culture that has now been subverted. This is pure romanticism, they argue. The reality is that for working men and women in pre-industrial society life was usually nasty, brutish and short. Modern society has made most people literate and this has enabled them to be discerning consumers of an ever-expanding cultural output. This includes not only literature in the conventional sense, but also TV and radio output, films, journalism and so on. People are also far more *politically* literate and aware of the world around them than was the case in the past. This allows them to appreciate, and choose from, a wide range of options.

Class distinctions have become less and less important in influencing the choices made by individuals in this respect. Members of the working class are as likely to be watching *Panorama* as anybody else, while soap operas are now appealing to the middle class as well as the working class.

In support of their arguments, pluralists point to the way in which even 'high culture' now reaches a mass audience. With the advent of TV and radio, drama music and opera have become accessible to more of the population than was ever the case in the past. The use made of these media by The Open University has additionally brought higher education to thousands who were unable to gain access to it before. The provision of public libraries has expanded the reading public. The greater affluence of the population in general has given the spare money for buying books and newspapers. Music recording and reproduction technology has developed very quickly in this century so that modern hi-fi systems with CD players and discs, DAT players and cassettes, as well as less esoteric (and cheaper) equipment are available to almost everyone. As well as this, one should take into account the expansion in the range of cultural output. Tastes of all sorts are catered for in virtually every area of output. Taking music as an illustration, there is easy access to the music of many nations as well as forms of music from Brahms to the Beatles, from Talking Heads to Toyah. An individual's collection is likely to contain a mixture of these. There is nothing intrinsically 'plastic' or false about the music, literature, films and so on of today. To say that there is is merely a form of snobbery. There are no objective standards to say that one is better than another. The individual simply has the freedom to make his or her choice based on personal preference.

☐ **The quote at the beginning of this section states that a fairly uniform pattern of mass media use now pervades the class structure. What method from those listed on page 19 could you most successfully use to put this idea to the test? Write about 200 words on how you would use your chosen method to test this hypothesis about class structure and media use.**

☐ **Construct an enlarged version of the following table with a short summary in each box:**

Table summarising the three perspectives on mass culture

	Conservative right	Radical left	Pluralism
What has been lost?			
Why?			
What is modern mass culture like?			
What effect does mass culture have?			

Table showing how culture can be ranked

	Books	Music
Good	Shakespeare	Beethoven
Mediocre	Jeffrey Archer	Beatles
Bad	Mills and Boon novels	Sex Pistols

Is it possible to rank art, literature and music in this way?
If it is, what makes Shakespeare 'better' than Archer?
If it isn't, is beauty simply in the eye of the beholder, with all of equal worth?

☐ **ESSAY**

... the modern best-seller is concerned with supporting herd prejudices ... the training of the reader who spends his leisure in cinemas, looking through magazines and newspapers, listening to jazz music, does not merely fail to help him, it prevents him from normal development. (Q.D. Leavis, Fiction and the Reading Public, *1932)*

[TV] ... dulls human sensibility, dims awareness of the world, encourages separation—people from communities, people from each other, people from themselves (J. Mander, Four Arguments for the Elimination of Television*)*

Explain and discuss the views expressed by these two authors.

☐ *Film is probably the most powerful propaganda medium yet devised. As a consequence its potential for aiding or injuring civilisation is enormous. (Agee, Ault and Emery,* Introduction to Mass Communications, *Harper and Row, 7th edition, 1982)*

How far would you agree with this view of film compared with, for example, the broadcast and published media?

Bibliography

A. Swingewood, *The Myth of Mass Culture*, Macmillan, London, 1977

B. Rosenberg, *Mass Culture*, Macmillan, London, 1965

D. McQuail, *The Sociology of Mass Communications*, Penguin, Harmondsworth, 1972

H. Gans, *Popular Culture and High Culture*, Basic Books, New York, 1974

C. Bigsby, (ed), *Approaches to Popular Culture*, Edward Arnold, London, 1976

R. Hoggart, *The Uses of Literacy*, Chatto and Windus, London, 1957

R. Williams, *Television, Technology and Cultural Form*, Collins, London, 1974

Open University Course, *Popular Culture*, U203, (terminated in 1987)

P. Johnson, *The Menace of Beatleism*, New Statesman, 28 February 1964

D. Bell, *The Coming of Post Industrial Society*

N. Jacobs, (ed), *Culture for the Millions?*, Beacon Press, Boston, 1964. The quote at the end of the section on the conservative right comes from O. Handlin, *Comments on Mass and Popular Culture*, pages 63–71 (in this text page 49).

J. Mander, *Four Arguments for the Elimination of Television*, Harvester Press, Brighton, 1980

This chapter addresses two issues. The first is whether the mass media produce deviant behaviour among their audiences. The second is the way in which the media portray deviance and deviants, the effects this portrayal has and the causes of it.

Deviance has been defined as 'disapproved behaviour which is so far outside the normal that it causes offence among the community at large'. A deviant is someone who acts in such a disapproved way. It should be noted here, though, that this definition is rather misleading. This is because it presumes that there is a 'community' who are unanimously repelled by a particular form of behaviour. This is not really the case; what is deviance to one person may seem normal or just eccentric to another.

☐ **List about five examples of behaviour to illustrate this point.**

The media as a cause of deviant behaviour

In Britain, Mary Whitehouse is a name associated with the 'moral majority' who are concerned about deviance in society and the influence of the media in increasing, even encouraging it. Sex and violence are themes which crop up quite frequently in this debate. Writing about children's comics, for example, Mrs Whitehouse believes that:

*'The Beano and the Dandy tend to give the impression that violence is all a big joke, that you can hit somebody on the head very hard and the next time you see them they are walking around as if nothing had happened' (*The Observer)

Mrs Whitehouse has come to symbolise conservative middle class Britain, defending old values from the pernicious influence of liberals and deviants in the media and elsewhere. She, and others like her, are quick to point to the similarities between the showing of such films as *Rambo* and events like the killing of sixteen people by the heavily armed Michael Ryan in Hungerford in August 1987. Their conclusion is that the media need to be carefully monitored and censored where necessary for the good of the community at large.

☐ **The bar chart and commentary below summarise the result of a survey carried out by the IBA in 1984 on public attitudes to potentially offensive items on TV. How do your attitudes compare to those of this sample of people?**
What about the attitudes of the group you are studying with?

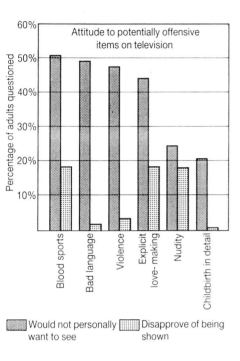

Would not personally want to see / Disapprove of being shown

In addition to its annual survey, the IBA commissioned one of its periodic special surveys on attitudes to matters of 'taste and decency' in the last year, preceding the survey with group discussions in six locations around the country. Arising out of the preliminary qualitative research, the survey asked about attitudes to six potentially offensive items or aspects of television broadcasting. Respondents were asked, first, if each item was something which 'you personally would not want to see', and then secondly, 'do you disapprove of it ... being shown on TV?'

The results are shown in the diagram and require no further comment. The results are from the complete sample, but there were strong differences within it: between the young and the old, and between men and women (except in the case of childbirth), but there were no social class differences. As will be seen, actual disapproval was expressed about only three items, and then by less than one in five of the respondents. The detailed results showed that it was women rather than men, and the old rather than the young, who disapproved of the portrayal of nudity and love-making. More disapproval of blood sports was expressed by men than by women, and by the young than by the old.

Source: IBA, Annual Report and Accounts 1984–5, p.50

Those, like Mrs Whitehouse, who believe that the media have a negative effect on behaviour use a number of arguments in support of their view. Firstly, they say that the mass media increase the general level of crime and deviance in society in the following ways:

Through prophecying trouble they create it and, additionally, amplify any deviance which may already exist

News and other factual programmes, by giving publicity to trouble spots and potential violence, actually cause that violence and trouble to occur. When this happens there has been a *self-fulfilling prophecy*. The South African government argued that this was occurring in its country and as a result introduced legislation which censored domestic and foreign media coverage of black unrest there. It also placed restrictions on the movement of journalists around the country. The presence of the media encouraged the blacks to riot because they knew they would have an audience, the argument runs. It was in recognition of this effect that British news editors some years ago decided to stop reporting a spate of bomb hoaxes which were plaguing airline companies. It was felt that the hoaxers were gaining satisfaction from the reports of their actions (planes delayed, searches of aircraft etc). The number of hoaxes was dramatically reduced following this decision. There are tales of camera crews, in search of good pictures, deliberately inciting violence so that they could get them. In Northern Ireland too there are said to have been occasions when foreign camera crews have encouraged young Catholic boys to throw stones at the army in front of the cameras.

The process of self-fulfilling prophecy occurs like this:

media reinforce and magnify threat of trouble
↓
consequent rumours and images solidify social groups
↓
cultural symbols become firm and understood by all
↓
participants learn how they are expected to behave
↓
hostility and preparedness for trouble spread among social groups
↓
groups cast as opponents become increasingly hostile
↓
trouble breaks out
↓
order is restored by police, courts and (sometimes) new legislation

Thus the mass media, almost single handed, have created deviance out of little or nothing (the process known as deviancy amplification) and, by predicting that something is going to happen, have made it happen (the self-fulfilling prophecy). Academic studies of this process occurring include Stan Cohen's *Folk Devils and Moral Panics* and Jock Young's *The Drugtakers*, though these both deal with events of some years ago. A more recent case occurred in 1985 and involved what was popularly known as the 'hippy convoy' (a phrase which itself has all sorts of associations—'labels'—attached to it). For more than a decade, festival people had been gathering at Stonehenge to celebrate the summer solstice. However, there had been an increasingly wide gulf between them and the rest of society, largely created by the media. Despite a history of peaceful celebration the police decided in 1985 to mount a massive operation against the 'hippies' which led to violent confrontation and, in effect, the creation of a problem where there had been none before; 'deviancy amplification'. Trouble was predicted as June approached in each of the subsequent years and a huge police operation was mounted to divert the festival people, whose determination to celebrate the festival had become even stronger.

☐ **These events are documented in an article by A. Rosenberger in *The Guardian*, 23 May 1986, amongst other places. Obtain a copy of the article and consider whether you agree with his interpretation of the events he describes in detail. Are there any similar examples of the self-fulfilling prophecy and deviancy amplification by the media that have occurred more recently? In thinking about this you should look for:**

● **detailed descriptions in the media of some deviant person or group**
● **description of some trouble that they have caused in the past**
● **a prediction of when and where they are likely to cause trouble again.**

By encouraging imitation of what is seen on the screen

Here the argument is that individuals, especially children, are likely to copy what they see on the screen. To continue the theme of rioting and 'trouble-spots' discussed above, after the riots in Liverpool and Brixton in the early 1980s, heavily reported in the media, there were a considerable number of other (so-called 'copycat') riots in towns around the country. Another example is newspaper stories of young killers or violent children who are addicted to video nasties like *Driller Killer*, *The Evil Dead*, *I Spit on Your Grave* etc. They became criminalised as a result of viewing these films, the theory goes.

A number of academic studies have been conducted and claim to show that imitation occurs, especially among children. Many of these have been conducted in laboratory conditions so that proof of an imitative effect can be established. Perhaps typical of these is the study by Bandura, Ross and Ross. They set up the experiment with four groups of children:

>   group 1 saw real-life male and female adults attacking a self-righting inflatable doll with mallets
>
>   group 2 saw a film of male and female adults attacking a self-righting inflatable doll with mallets
>
>   group 3 saw a TV film of cartoon characters attacking a self-righting inflatable doll with mallets
>
>   group 4 was the control group. They saw no violent activity.

Following this experience each individual child was deliberately mildly frustrated by being put in a room with a lot of exciting toys but, on beginning to play with them, being told that they were reserved for other children. The child was then put in a room with a doll like those seen by groups 1, 2 and 3. Each child spent twenty minutes in this room being observed by judges seated behind a one-way mirror. They recorded the behaviour of the child, response measures included imitative aggression, partially imitative aggression, mallet aggression, sitting on the doll, non-imitative aggression and aggressive gun play. Bandura *et al* concluded that:

> ... *aggressive behaviour was sharply higher in each of the model conditions in comparison with the control, and further, that most of this difference was due to the direct imitation of the model's aggressive behaviours. Differences between the various viewing conditions—live, film, and television—were negligible.*

Recently many people have become concerned about the influence of the new breed of American cartoons which have been screened in Britain since 1983. Examples include *He-Man*, *Go-Bots* and *Thunder Cats*. Imitation of these is seen as particularly undesirable because they:

- portray the goodies using violence to defeat baddies

- do not show the unpleasant effects of that violence (the baddies never die)

- give status to characters merely on the basis of strength and fighting ability

- encourage imitation of the hero characters through the sale of associated merchandise (swords, clothing etc). Violence is, therefore, being positively promoted

- portray women in a very stereotyped way while the white male heroes are ridiculously macho. Sexist attitudes and behaviour are, therefore, reinforced

- associate evil with blackness and a sense of 'foreign-ness'. Violence towards blacks is thus condoned.

In addition, they are not primarily designed as entertainment at all. They have poor characterisation, bad artwork and almost non-existent storylines. They are, in effect, merely advertising. *He-Man*, for example, was a toy produced by Mattel who then approached Filmation of California to make a cartoon about the character which would then be syndicated to the American TV networks. Mattel and Filmation are in constant touch about storylines, new characters etc. An attempt is always made to include in each episode every character currently on sale in order to maintain awareness of and desire for each of them. Thus, two profit-motivated corporations are cynically manipulating children with no regard for the effects of their products on the children themselves or the future of society as a whole, the argument goes.

By de-sensitising the audience to violence and other forms of deviance

This theory says that watching violence on television arouses children especially, making them excited. However, the more they watch, the more extreme must the violence be to arouse them. The result is that they become de-sensitised to it and are not shocked by real life violence as they may once have been.

This argument applies particularly to video nasties. In these films the level of violence is so great that more usual forms of violence seem mild by comparison. According to the authors of The British Parliamentary Group Video Enquiry, such films lose their power to shock after repeated exposure and the viewer finds it necessary to search for greater and greater levels of violence. Of particular concern to them, as to others, is the violence against women which most of this genre of film contains. Violent rape, especially, is a constant theme in them, and the danger is that such events, either fictional or in real life, no longer shock or repel the individual.

Through eroding inbuilt inhibitions about acting in certain ways ('disinhibition')

This suggests that the inhibitions about sexual or violent behaviour are broken down if such behaviour is portrayed as 'normal' on the screen. This is particularly likely to happen if deviant behaviour goes unpunished in films.

Feminists, in particular, are concerned about the media's treatment of women in this respect. The *Women's Monitoring Network*, based in London, reviews this and other aspects of media production. They argue that:

> *'Society generally abhors violence and yet violence against women is both treated as commonplace and exploited for its news and entertainment value and marketability. This not only reflects current social attitudes but serves also to reinforce and encourage acceptance of them.' (Report no. 2* Violence Against Women)

These arguments are supported by both field studies and laboratory studies of the effects of violence on the screen. We saw earlier that the laboratory study by Bandura *et al* found an imitative effect after viewing violence on the screen. A field study which supports the case that media violence causes actual violence is W. Belson's *Television Violence and the Adolescent Boy*. He carried out fieldwork with interviews of 1,565 London boys between the ages of twelve and seventeen. A central feature of the study was for the boys to sort cards which carried different statements about violence (eg, 'I have thrown something at someone'; 'I have given someone a head butt'). Belson's study is unusual in that it tries to establish not just that boys who watch violent TV also commit violent acts themselves, but that the former *caused* the latter. This is done by conducting a long-term study of both behaviour and viewing preferences, partly by asking the boys to think about their past behaviour and viewing so that it can be established which came first. He also tries to get round the problems of defining exactly what 'violence' is by delineating no less than twenty-two different kinds of behaviour, from swearing and abuse to very serious physical violence. The conclusion of the study was that children who tend to watch violent TV programmes do become more violent themselves to some extent, largely because violence comes to be seen as a legitimate problem-solving device for them.

Let us conclude the case against the media. The rapid growth of the mass media, and, particularly, the spread of the use of VCRs in Britain (UK has a higher density of VCRs per head of the population than any other nation) gives great cause for concern. A NSPCC survey conducted in December 1983 and January 1984 showed that 36.7 per cent of children had seen at least one film which could be roughly categorised as a 'video nasty'. A National Viewers' Survey of a representative sample of 4,500 children between seven and sixteen years published in 1984 yielded similar results. 45 per cent of them had seen a 'video nasty' and the children's favourite viewing in the '18' rated category tended to be horror, occult or pornographic films. Unlike fiction in earlier eras, the video film is often sexually explicit, there is gratuitous violence and it is no longer the case that good triumphs over evil, rather the reverse. The evidence and argument that we have examined above show conclusively that the mass media do have bad effects, particularly on young and impressionable people. Small wonder that in a survey of 404 consultants and senior registrars working in the field of child and adolescent psychiatry, 81.2 per cent of those who responded considered that video was an important factor in their patients' lives prior to the survey. 50.5 per cent of those who responded thought that there was an association between their patients' symptoms and viewing violent videos. Similar results were found in a survey of paediatricians and reports by teachers. One of the latter wrote:

> '*I (and my colleagues) are becoming increasingly alarmed at the way young children are given access to "X" rated video films. We have noticed that children who watch such films become very nervous, excessively bite fingernails and become withdrawn. One infant child who was exposed to pornographic material became very disruptive and violent.*'

Mrs Whitehouse, herself a retired teacher, recounts a similar instance:

Which of the following, if any, should or should definitely *not* be the subject of censorship?: TV programmes, books, magazines, video films, cinema films.

If you believe that any of them should be censored, try drafting a paragraph of a law to set the limits on what can be shown. If you are working in a group, swap your 'law' with another person in the group. Do you agree with their law? Is it more restrictive than yours or less so? Are there any loopholes in it? Which is the better of the two?
(A brief quote from the present law, the **Obscene Publications Act**, is included in a note at the end of this chapter for comparison with your version.)

'We were talking [in class] one day about the effects of fear in horrific programmes and films. What actually did such programmes do to people? "I know what happens to me, miss," said one normally happy-go-lucky soul, "I become so tired with fright that anyone could do anything with me." '

Despite the passing of the Video Recordings Act in 1984 (which restricted what could be hired from video shops and imposed a categorisation system on video films) children are still able to get access to video nasties. Even video *games* such as Space Invaders and Roadrunner have been found to raise the level of aggressive play, and to lower the level of pro-social play in five year old children. As the capacity of computers increases and their graphics capability expands there are disturbing possibilities in the area of sex role stereotyping. One popular game at the moment is Strip Poker, which involves fairly poor digitised pictures of Sam Fox stripping as she loses the card game to the player. Development of this theme has so far only been hindered by the poor quality of computer graphics.

Censorship needs to be introduced so that children can grow up in a decent atmosphere, women be treated other than as sexual objects to be used and abused and violence not be seen as the norm. While this may be seen as an infringement of civil liberties by some, it is a small and necessary price to pay for the good of society as a whole.

Those who reject the view that the media amplify the level of deviance in society argue that the case that they increase the amount of crime and deviance is not proven. This is so for the following reasons:

1 Because laboratory studies like that described above are all unreliable. The reasons for this are elaborated on page 27.

2 Field studies examining the relationship between media violence and real violence are both ambivalent in their results and as unreliable as laboratory studies. This unreliability is due to the following problems:

- The methodology employed in field studies is never precise enough to establish a proven link between viewing violent programmes and films and subsequent deviant behaviour. The causes of a person's actions are many, various and difficult to identify, even by the person performing them. For an academic researcher to say that a particular behaviour was caused by exposure to the portrayal of deviance on the media is, at best, a guess. Even Belson's impressive research, which takes into account 227 possibly relevant variables which may affect violent behaviour, still may have overlooked other relevant variables such as subtle aspects of the personality.

- Those studies that do claim to establish a correlation between TV viewing and violent behaviour are really only showing that violent people enjoy violent programmes. It's not really worth spending a lot of time, money and effort to state such an obvious fact. Belson tried to get round this problem of cause and effect by asking the boys he interviewed to remember past behaviour and viewing habits. Unfortunately this procedure leaves plenty of room for forgetfulness, selective recall and plain lies.

- It is far from clear what constitutes violence, in the media or in real life. The perception of violence in a programme is a subjective assessment. There is disagreement as to whether violence in *fictional* programmes has more, or less, impact than *real* violence shown on the news. Perhaps violence in cartoons cannot be counted as violence at all because there is no attempt to make the characters 'real' in any sense. Also, it is not clear how far children are able to distinguish between what is and is not real in what they see on the TV screen. Perhaps the most important point, though, is the fact that the critics of the mass media grossly exaggerate the amount of sex and violence on TV. While there may be more on video and at the cinema, one must make a positive effort to seek it out, which implies an initial taste for it.

- There are at least as many studies of media violence which discover no effect on behaviour as do discover an effect. One example is Hilde Himmelweit and her colleagues who studied 4,500 children from English cities. Some of the children lived in homes with TVs, others without (this was in the early days of television when reception was not possible in much of the country). They carefully matched four groups of children in this way:

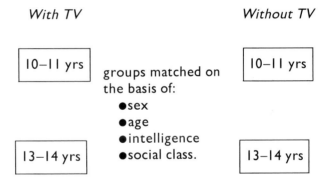

Questionnaires were given before and after a six week period and teachers were asked to rate children's behaviour and personality. The influence of TV was found to be:

> *'... far less colourful and dramatic than popular opinion is inclined to suppose ... whether TV is good or bad for children depends on the programmes, the amount the child views, the type of child, the type of effects to be examined and the context in which viewing takes place.'*

Similar results were obtained by Schramm *et al* in a major series of studies conducted in the USA and Canada between 1958 and 1960. Eleven studies were carried out in all, involving interviews with a total of 6,000 students, 2,000 parents, several hundred teachers, officials and other knowledgeable people. In some cases, questionnaires and the completion of diaries by the subjects were also used. The conclusion was that delinquency and violence are complex phenomena with a number of roots and that TV is, at best, only a contributory cause:

> *No informed person can say simply that TV is bad or that it is good for children.*

☐ **If you are working in a classroom situation try the following exercise.**
Working alone, answer the following questions:

- **What is the most violent programme or event that you have seen on TV?**

- **What was your reaction to it?**

- **Should it have been shown?**

- **What was the most sexually explicit episode you have seen on TV?**

- **Should it have been shown in that form, edited or not shown at all?**

- **Do you feel that either had any influence on you?**

Compare your answers to those of the rest of the group.

For some children, under some conditions, or for the same children under other conditions, it may be beneficial. For most children, under most conditions, most TV is probably neither particularly harmful nor particularly beneficial.

Finally, a field study of 816 children conducted by P. Edgar in Australia concluded that:

In the study . . . I found that the children in the sample made more sophisticated discriminations about mass media content than many people assume children are capable of. . . . When talking about 13 year olds it can be said:
1. *It is the context of violence not the nature or extent of the violence that is important to children. As long as the rules of a western, crime film or war film are complied with, violence is acceptable and understood.*
2. *What disturbs children is something that relates to their own experience that they can identify with—and that something will differ for each child.*
3. *Children interpret film and television content differently from adults.*
4. *Children believe the news, and films which are simulated to look like news.*

Generally, those who believe that the media provoke deviant behaviour have a naïve and outdated view of how the media work. They tend to adopt the hypodermic model of media effects. This suggests that the media transmit a message which is 'injected' into the audience and, like a drug, changes them in some way. Serious analysts of the media have now moved beyond this model. They recognise that the audience consists not of a homogeneous mass but of individuals and groups. These watch, read or listen for different reasons, with different degrees of attentiveness and understanding and with different preconceptions. Any influence on them will not be constant, nor will it affect them all in the same way. Different people will be affected in different ways, or not at all. The simplistic use of the hypodermic model is illustrated in the following quote from the *Women's Monitoring Network*'s report *Women as Sex Objects*:

[The media] constantly present women as glamorous, alluring and available. This results in women being viewed as objects, to be used for the pleasure and profit of men. Inevitably, men's attitudes towards women are influenced by this voyeuristic approach.

There is nothing inevitable about it. Many men are able to dismiss for what it is the sort of fiction referred to in the quote. More sophisticated analyses, adopting a uses and gratifications approach (such as Schramm's), are far more equivocal in their results.

Some of those who wish to defend the media go beyond this critique of the available evidence and suggest that the amount of crime and deviance can be actually *reduced* thanks to the media. This is done by:

Releasing tension and desires through identification with fictional characters and events (catharsis)

Catharsis is the release or dissipation of strong emotion. The cathartic effect has long been recognised. Psychiatrists have used it in the treatment of sex offenders by showing them blue movies to help them release their emotions. Films like *Rambo* and *Death Wish* could have a positive effect on those individuals with violent impulses by helping them to release them through identification with the hero of the film.

Sensitising people to the effects of violence

Exposure to violence and other forms of deviance not normally encountered in everyday life is just as likely to make people more sensitive to it as the reverse. Bloody scenes of the consequences of violence and war (such as those in the film *Platoon*) often shock and revolt people so much that their attitudes are hardened against acting like this. As far as crime in general is concerned, sensitisation to certain types of crime can make people more aware of it and more likely to report it. Child abuse cases, recently highlighted in the media, have heightened public consciousness of the problem and increased the rate of reporting of cases to the police and other agencies.

Taking the specific points made about programmes such as *He-Man* and the like, their defenders reject the claim that they are harmful in any way. Lou Sheimer, President of Filmation, argues that:

- the heroes act co-operatively in groups and this is a good model for children
- that racism and sexism are avoided. There are female heroines behaving in a strong, self-reliant way. Black villains are deliberately not introduced. He-Man's arch-rival, Skeletor, is *purple*.
- *He-Man* takes up only a small part of the child's day; other influences on behaviour are far more important
- children know that *He-Man* is imaginary
- *Tom and Jerry* were far more violent and had no storyline to speak of, yet the very people complaining about *He-Man* watched and enjoyed those cartoons with no ill-effects. The critique is merely a disguised form of conservatism.
- there is a large amount of self-mockery in the *He-Man* Programme. It is tongue-in-cheek.

☐ **Watch one episode of *He-Man* (or similar cartoon) and prepare a report on its content. Issues you may wish to consider are:**

- **how much violence is used?**
- **are the effects of violence shown?**
- **is violence used to solve problems in the programme and is its use applauded?**
- **is there harmonious cooperation between the 'goodies'?**
- **are there any reasons given for the heroes being seen as good, other than their superior force?**

Let us now conclude the case for the defence. Surveys of children such as those quoted earlier are notoriously unreliable. Kids are inclined to say they have seen video nasties they haven't. This was shown by researchers studying five classes of eleven year olds who were given the National Viewers Survey questionnaire referred to above. The only difference was that titles of films which did not exist were inserted. 68 per cent of the children claimed to have seen these

☐ **Thinking about violence you have seen on TV, do you feel that in *your* case it:**
a) **desensitised you to violence**
b) **sensitised you to violence**
c) **neither**
d) **the effect depended on the extent of violence, how it was portrayed, whether the victim was portrayed and how, etc, (specify what)?**

☐ **Imagine that you had been offered a grant of, say, £20,000 to research the question 'to what extent do video films make young people more likely to commit sexual or violent offences?'**

    1. **What problems can you see with the project remit as it stands? (Make any amendments to the aim of the research project that you want, within reason).**

    2. **How would you go about researching this so that you would have some plausible empirical results for your sponsors?**

☐ **Draw up guidelines for TV drama writers on writing violent scenes on TV. You might consider whether they should be graphic and show the victim sympathetically (in order to sensitise people to the effects of violence); how much should be shown, where the limits are, and so on.**

films! Surveys of professionals, too, are really discovering no more than their personal view; they have no real idea about the influence the media may be having on people. The truth is that the media can have a positive effect. They may sensitise children and others to violence and deviance, they may help to release violent emotions. In terms of intellectual skills, too, the influence can often be a beneficial one. This is true even of the much-criticised cartoon programmes. Bob Hodge and David Tripp in *Children and Television* suggest that TV viewing is not a passive, mindless activity, but one which develops a number of cognitive skills in children. In watching a programme even as apparently simple as the American cartoons, children are actively interpreting and constructing meanings. (Hodge and Tripps' findings are discussed in more detail on page 23.) This conclusion is supported by C. Cullingford's analysis of the results of a survey of use of the media by over 5,000 children from many backgrounds in the US and the UK. He writes:

> '*Children are capable of intense appreciation and the closest critical scrutiny. They can be absorbed in a story and learn new information rapidly and efficiently. No account of children's responses should ignore this fact by being trapped into an over-simple generalisation. . . . This proof of children's ability to attend to the intended message of the programme contrasts with some of the research evidence that gives an impression that children are being moulded into imitators of violence or into passive and inarticulate zombies.*'

So the violence on TV is not only not harmful to children (they are easily able to distinguish it from real violence)—it is beneficial in that it helps them to develop these cognitive skills and to 'read' the plot of the programme. Violence acts as a signifier of conflict and difference, and as such it is essential to allow its portrayal in children's programmes and elsewhere. Without it not only TV cartoon programmes but part of the past and present would be seriously impoverished.

Images of deviance in the media

This section will examine three aspects of the media representation of deviance and deviants:

- How the media portrays deviance
- The causes of this representation
- The effects it has on the deviants and on society as a whole.

The media portrayal of deviance

Social scientists have formulated the following hypotheses on this issue:

Some sorts of deviance are highlighted and exaggerated in the media, others are ignored

The media are very selective in which aspects of deviance they portray. The following are the beginnings of the lists of types of deviance which are over- and under-reported respectively:

	Over-reported	Under-reported
	Drugs	*Drugs*
	Cocaine abuse	Alcohol abuse
	Marijuana abuse	Tobacco abuse
	Glue sniffing	Food additives
	Crime	*Crime*
	Sex crime	Fraud and general white-collar crime
	Violent crime	Theft and handling stolen goods

☐ **Continue these two lists by adding other types of deviance that are under- and over-reported.**

On the question of the media's selectivity on drug reporting, Jock Young has developed what he calls his *Law of Information on Drugs.* This runs: 'The greater the health risk (as measured by the number of deaths) of a drug, the less the amount of information critical of its effects there will be in the media'.

He makes the point that alcohol and tobacco kill far more people than other, illegal, drugs. However, because they are used for relaxation and recuperation after work and don't disturb the individual's productivity, they are accepted. Nancy Reagan's heavily reported *Just Say No* campaign, designed to stop young people getting involved with cocaine, etc, made no mention of these. Only the drugs which threaten profitability are given media prominence.

Deviants are seen as being on the fringe of society

The media propagate the view that the vast bulk of the population are completely "normal". They are not trade unionists. They never go on strike. They hold no radical or militant political views. They are not feminists. They do not join movements like CND. They enjoy consumption for its own sake. They live in nuclear families and so on.

Figure A shows the general media view of society.

However, when there are mass disturbances, such as the miners' strike in 1985–6 or the Winter of Discontent in 1978–9, this model is no longer sufficient (it doesn't explain why there is so much support for the 'deviant' action) so a more sophisticated model has to be introduced (Figure B).

A small number of deviants are blamed for social problems: they act as scapegoats

For example, local government bodies which disagree with spending cuts by central government are seen as being in the hands of the Militant Tendency. This small and shadowy organisation is blamed for what the media sees as crazy policies when in fact these councils have been elected by popular vote and there is widespread support for their policies. Individuals, too, are often identified as the prime trouble makers (see the front page of *The Sun* on page 88). Ken Livingstone, Tony Benn and Derek Hatton (ex-deputy leader of Liverpool Council) have all been cast in this role. They become *folk devils*: the subject of universal abuse and hatred whipped up by the media, particularly the tabloid press.

Deviant movements and forces become personalised. Their aims are forgotten by the media

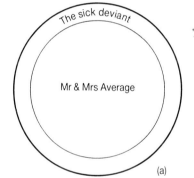

(a)

(b)

For example, militant unionism in Northern Ireland becomes personified by Ian Paisley who is then ridiculed as a ranting senseless bigot, effectively ridiculing the whole movement. This can be a very effective means of moulding the public's attitudes towards quite complex issues, whether deliberately or not.

□ **What other examples of the personification of deviant movements can you identify?**

The 'Nemesis Effect': the media show us that those who deviate from the social norms always suffer for it in the long run

Nemesis was the Greek Goddess of retribution who ensured that evil-doers were punished. Thus the 'Nemesis Effect' in the media is the way the media show us that this happens to deviants of all sorts. This applies to drugs:

LSD: THE FLY NOW, DIE LATER DRUG
(The *Chicago American*).

It also applies to criminals (the cops always get their man/woman in fiction and usually on the news and *Crimewatch* too). Most recently it has applied to homosexuals. The AIDS scare and the media's concentration on its effects on the homosexual community and their sexual practices illustrate the Nemesis Effect in action. Indeed some have argued that AIDS is literally divine retribution for the unnatural practices of gays.

□ **Have there been any recent examples of the Nemesis Effect in the broadcast news or the press?**

Deviants are sometimes portrayed as being 'just normal people underneath'

This occurs when deviants appear to threaten the status quo in society and is an alternative reaction to the *moral panic* one. The media respond by turning that deviance into a 'leisure-time only' activity. Punks, for example, are portrayed in the press as just normal kids underneath—they go to school and worry about exams like anyone else. Their parents are Mr and Mrs Average. Their clothes become high fashion and are soon to be found on the racks of the High Street stores. This can occur in the media itself. *Rolling Stone*, the American music paper founded in the 60s was once an alternative and radical publication. It adopted a questioning and threatening stance, rejecting the accepted values. Today it is much more sedate. It even carries recruitment advertisements for the armed services. Threatening deviance both outside and within the media, then, is neutralised and incorporated into the system.

The effects of the media's distorted representation of deviants and deviance

The amplification of deviance

This refers to the idea that, by exaggerating the extent and nature of deviance and by giving it publicity, the media actually increase its level. Deviance is created where there was none before. Where it existed before the level of deviance is increased. People are drawn into deviance who were not deviant before. These processes and how they operate have already been dealt with earlier in the chapter. Academic studies of this effect in operation include S. Cohen's *Folk Devils and Moral Panics* and J. Young's *The Drugtakers.* The former showed how Mods and Rockers were virtually created by the media through largely fictional accounts of violent incidents at South Coast resorts. The latter demonstrated how Notting Hill marijuana users were criminalised and forced into greater deviance by media exaggeration of their behaviour and lifestyle and subsequent police action against them.

Social control

Social control means preventing people behaving and thinking in abnormal or deviant ways. This acts in the opposite direction to the amplification of deviance. However, there need not be a contradiction here. The media reporting of deviance can amplify it among a small social group (say, drug takers or some young people) while at the same time having the effect of social control on the rest of us. Stan Cohen argues this in *Folk Devils and Moral Panics*, as do other authors. The media act as an agency of social control through the use of the Nemesis Effect, the manipulation of the general public's attitudes towards deviance of all sorts and the other distortions of 'deviant behaviour'. The audience is dissuaded from following the deviants' example and, implicitly, threatened with the consequences of so doing. Social control is also achieved through the containment of deviant movements by incorporating them into the establishment. By treating deviant movements as 'just a fad' and their members as 'really just normal people going through a phase' and by commercialising the artefacts of deviant movements, the media effectively neutralise them as a threat to the established system.

The causes of the media's distorted view of deviants and deviance

Manipulative theory argues that those in the media, who represent the political and economic establishment, deliberately distort deviance in the ways we have examined. This is done in order to strengthen the status quo, ensuring that 'normality' continues and those who threaten it are marginalised and ridiculed in the public mind.

Hegemonic theory, which is subscribed to by far more writers, argues that this process is an unconscious one. Those in the media unwittingly portray deviants and deviance in this way because their lives and behaviour are so foreign to the average journalist. Journalists unconsciously use concepts of newsworthiness and public interest which are derived from the viewpoint of the dominant class(es) in society. They genuinely see society as based on fundamental consensus, with only a few sick or evil people not adhering to the consensual view. They cannot recognise the frustrations and rejection of society that can lead to deviance; they have never felt such emotions. So, they genuinely believe that deviants must be sick, stupid, mindless, gullible or 'just normal really'.

Pluralist theory states that in the area of deviance, as with the others we have examined, the media are giving the public what they want. People *like* to see the good guy win and the bad guy lose. They are comforted by the belief that the police always, or at least usually, catch the criminal. The pluralists agree that the facts are that the police only rarely do so, especially with some types of crime such as burglary, particularly in inner city areas, but people don't want to know this. It would only make the public uneasy if the media insisted on telling them harsh facts such as these and the only noticeable effect would be a decline in sales and viewing figures.

Conservatives like Mrs Whitehouse, however, would disagree with the academics on many issues concerning the media and deviance. They believe, first, that the media often treat deviance approvingly. Second, and as a result, they believe that the media encourage deviance not only among certain social groups but the population as a whole. Conservatives consider that too often deviance is shown as going unpunished on TV and in video films. For conservatives, then, the effect of the media is to *promote* deviance, but not to operate social control.

☐ **ESSAY**

To what extent are the mass media implicated in the process of deviancy amplification?

Note

The present Obscene Publications Act (1959) outlaws material which is 'obscene'. Something is 'obscene' if . . .

'its effect . . . is . . . such as to deprave and corrupt persons who are likely . . . to read, see or hear the material contained in it'

Juries decide whether this is the case or not in each instance.

Bibliography

C. Lodziak, *The Power of Television: a critical appraisal*, Pinter, London, 1987

R. Clutterbuck, *The Media and Political Violence*, Macmillan, London, 1983

Observer, 9 June, 1987, *Chomp! Thatcher Tucks into Cow Pie Capers*, page 5

S. Cohen, *Folk Devils and Moral Panics*, Martin Robertson, Oxford, 1980 (second edition)

The Women's Monitoring Network publications are available from the Women's Monitoring Network c/o A Woman's Place, Hungerford House, Victoria Embankment, London WC2

G. Barlow and A. Hill, (eds), *Video Violence and Children*, Hodder and Stoughton, London, 1985 (source of the quote (page 143) and the survey results)

B. Hodge and D. Tripp, *Children and Television*, Basil Blackwell, Oxford, 1985

C. Cullingford, *Children and TV*, Gower Publishers, Aldershot, 1984, quote in text from page 177

W. Schramm, *et al*, *Television and the Lives of Our Children*, Stanford University Press, Stanford, 1961. The quote in the text is from page 1

H. Himmelweit, *Television and the Child*, Oxford University Press, London, 1958. The quote in the text is from Himmelweit, *Television and the Child*, in B. Berelson and M. Janowitz, *Reader in Public Opinion and Communication*, The Free Press, New York, pp. 418–45.

W. Belson, *Television Violence and the Adolescent Boy*, Gower Press, Aldershot, 1978

A. Bandura, D. Ross and S.A. Ross, *The Imitation of Film-Mediated Aggressive Models*, Journal of Abnormal and Social Psychology, 66(1)3–11

H.J. Eysenck and D.K. Nias, *Sex, Violence and the Media*, Maurice Temple Smith, London, 1978

M. Whitehouse, *Cleaning Up Television*, Blandford Press, London, 1967

P. Edgar, *Children and Screen Violence*, University of Queensland Press, St Lucia, 1977

S. Cohen and J. Young, *The Manufacture of News: Social Problems, Deviance and the Mass Media*, Constable, London, 1973

S. Cohen, *Images of Deviance*, Penguin, Harmondsworth, 1971.

S. Moore, *Investigating Deviance*, Sociology in Action series, Unwin Hyman, London, 1988 (See especially chapter 4 for Moore's discussion of deviance and the media)

6 · Advertising and the Media

Advertisements are often ignored in the sociological study of the media. This omission is strange as it is only BBC television and radio among all the media which, for the moment at least, do not have them. The lack of attention to advertisements is perhaps explained by the sociologist's desire not to be associated with market research, the kind of enquiry paid for by, and conducted in the interests of, the manufacturers and suppliers of services.

There is a need to include the study of advertisements in any examination of the mass media, however. This is because, first, many commentators believe that they can be an important influence on the content of the media. Second, advertisements are clearly designed to influence our attitudes and behaviour where much other media output is not. Where better, then, to study whether the media has the power to affect us in these ways? Third, by ignoring the presence of advertisements, arguments become distorted. For example, the manipulative model of the media (see pages 33–37) gains considerable weight if one takes advertising content into account. Conversely, the pluralist's criticism (page 43) that in socialist countries where the media are manipulated the printed and broadcast information is positive and happy, whereas ours is negative and full of trauma, carries less weight. As *The New York Evening Post* recognised as far back as 1909 ...

> *In the magazine proper everything goes askew. The railroads cheat us and kill us. The food manufacturers poison us ... Workmen go without work ... The list is endless. But what a reconstructed world of heart's desire begins with the first-page advertisement. Here no breakfast food fails to build up a man's brain and muscle ... No razor cuts the face or leaves it sore ... Worry flies before the face of the model fountain pen ... Babies never cry ... A happy world indeed ...*

In discussing the importance of advertising in the media there are two important areas for us to examine:

1. How advertisements affect the audience
2. The impact on the mass media (ie, structure, content etc)

1. How advertisements affect the audience

It is commonly stated in the textbooks that nobody really knows whether, or how far, advertisements change people's attitudes towards products and brands, or even how far they encourage people to buy an advertised product. It is certainly unclear whether advertising increases total sales of goods or simply encourages the consumer to buy one brand rather than another. However, in view of the fact that £4,441 million was spent on advertising in Britain alone in 1985 it would seem that the companies which commission the advertisements have no doubt. Details from companies about their sales figures before and after an advertising campaign are the most obvious way of judging the effectiveness of advertising. Kellogg's television advertising of *Super Noodles* in 1979–80 achieved an increase in brand awareness of 23 per cent over the period November 1979 to October 1980 among housewives surveyed and a doubling (from 5 per cent to 10 per cent) of the numbers of housewives who said they had ever bought the product. Repeat purchasing of *Super Noodles* also increased following the TV campaign. The effectiveness of British Telecom's 'It's for yoo–hoo' series of advertisements was also tested, though in a different way. The aim of the advert was to encourage people to use the 'phone more. BT monitored the number of 'phone calls made after the advert on three occasions. Unfortunately, they refused to divulge the results of the test, but shortly afterwards they changed their advertising agency and switched to a different type of advert (in which animals make 'phone calls). We can probably assume that it showed this particular advert not to be effective.

For the purposes of academics, though, these studies present some problems. First, as in the BT example, the figures are usually kept confidential by companies. Second, they would only reveal the effectiveness or otherwise of the particular campaign to which they relate, not of advertising in general.

Advertising agencies have an obvious interest in persuading their clients of the effectiveness of advertising before a campaign is launched, and over the years they have developed quite sophisticated ideas about how advertisements work. We will look at some of these.

The earliest theory of advertising derived from the behaviourist school of psychology which assumed that people, like animals, respond in an automatic and predictable way to stimuli. Thus, it was believed that advertising worked in the following simple way:

ADVERTISING > CONSUMER > SALES

The use of simple catch phrases mark this sort of advertising.

"Good morning, have you used Pear's soap?"

was an early one (late nineteenth century) devised by Thomas Barratt to cash in on a phrase ('good morning') that would be used every day. This was so successful that it became impossible to hear the words 'good morning' without the phrase 'have you used Pear's soap' springing, unwelcome, into the mind. Such catch-phrases are still used today ('if you see Sid, tell him', for the sale of gas shares in 1986) and when set to music they can be unforgettable for the generation exposed to them ('you'll wonder where the yellow went when you wash your teeth with Pepsodent').

However, this approach ignored the role of the emotions and the subjective perception of advertisements, so the second mode was developed that looked like this:

☐ **Identify more up-to-date advertisements that use this sort of catch-phrase**

AWARENESS > INTEREST > DESIRE > SALES

This was the unfortunately-named AIDS model (so called because of the first letters of the steps involved). It assumed a rational action on the part of the consumer who took in the ad, remembered it and eventually bought the product. It led to a fashion in so-called 'reason why' advertising. An early example (1909) by H. Gordon Selfridge who was determined that his about-to-open store must have equal status with Harrods, etc, within seven days of opening ran:

> *The Great Principles upon which we will build this Business are as everlasting as the Pyramids. These Principles are Integrity, Truthfulness, Value-giving, Progressiveness, Dignity, Liberality, Courtesy, Originality, a daily presentation of what is New, coupled with a determination to Satisfy.*

Examine the current issue of three monthly magazines of different sorts. Find the relative numbers of ads using the AIDS approach and the attitude modification approach. Attempt to identify the reasons for the different sorts of advertisements in these magazines.

However, research showed that recall of a particular ad isn't very important in influencing the decision to buy (subliminal advertising, using rapidly flashed messages on screens or oral messages not consciously heard works despite the fact that the consumer isn't even aware of the ad). So, in the 1960s advertising agencies tried to encourage positive attitudes towards particular aspects of the brand. Thus, the aim was now to *modify attitudes.* Recently, multinational companies have started to adopt this approach in TV advertising (for example British Petroleum), trying to improve their corporate image among the British public, especially if a takeover bid is imminent.

Again, however, research evidence showed that advertising doesn't really work very well in this respect. Making the purchase and using the product appear to be at least as important in influencing attitudes as the advertising itself. If the product doesn't give satisfaction it is unlikely that the advertisement will persuade us to like it or the company which makes it.

The most recent model of how advertising works is closely linked to the 'uses and gratifications' approach to media influence (see page 28). It holds that people use advertisements rather than advertisements using people. Not everyone is interested in a particular product or service, thus, agencies need to *target* their audiences (ie, make sure the ad reaches the sort of people who might buy the product). Also the advertising strategy should be appropriate to the needs and interest of the people it is aimed at *and* to the nature of the product. Thus, 'reason why' advertising should be used for some types of product (say a car), whereas advertising appealing to the emotions or the senses should be used for others (say perfume).

Type of purchase		*Examples*
day to day convenience	*'trivial'*	tea, bread
occasional convenience		shoe polish
minor luxury		after shave
small durable		kettle, iron
major durable	*'serious'*	car, washing machine

This model requires agencies to conduct careful research into the potential market for the products they are working on. That market can be described in terms of a number of important characteristics. Social grade is one of the most crucial variables in this respect. To measure it agencies use the following scale:

Table 6.1:   *Measurement of social grade*

Grade	Occupation	% in pop^N/1986
A	Higher managerial, administrative and professional	3.1%
B	Intermediate managerial, administrative and professional	13.4%
C1	Supervisory or clerical and junior managerial, administrative and professional	22.3%
C2	Skilled manual	31.2%
D	Semi-skilled and unskilled manual	19.1%
E	Casual labourers, state pensioners, the unemployed	10.9%

Age is also important and agencies normally use the following groupings:

$$-15 \quad 15-24 \quad 24-35 \quad 35-55 \quad 55+$$

Some advertising agencies have adopted what they call a psychometric approach to the market. Instead of simply using scales of social class, they also try to measure attitudes and classify according to this dimension. Interviewers ask people whether they agree or disagree with statements like:

I always go to the same holiday resort because it is familiar
I think things used to be better than they are now
I think that people who do not have children are selfish.

Different sorts of people can be identified as a result of the analysis of answers, these being close to the commonly used categories of yuppie, preppie, and so on (though probably not 'lombard'—loads of money but a right d***!) with their associated attitudes. It is useful to be able to identify (for example) attitudinally experimental people so that the impact of advertising campaigns for a new type of product (like *Super Noodles*) can be tested on them.

☐ **The advertising content of three magazines was sampled by Vestergaard and Schroder. The magazines were *Playboy*, *Cosmopolitan* and *Woman*. Study the table below and decide which is X, which Y and which Z:**

Product	Percentage of advertisements		
	Magazine X	Magazine Y	Magazine Z
Hygiene	26	10	3
Beauty	39	18	1
Clothes	7	12	14
Household implements	2	18	–
Food, detergents	5	31	–
Tobacco	6	8	15
Beer, spirits	3	–	25
Leisure	3	–	5
Technological toys	2	–	38
Employment	3	–	–
Investment insurance	3	2	–

Source: Vestergaard and Schroder, p. 74.

In what ways have the readership of these magazines been 'targetted' by advertisers?

The answers are at the end of this chapter's bibliography.

☐ **List the sorts of advertisements which appear in *The Times* and *The Sun* in any one day. Construct a similar table. Identify the differences and comment on the different markets they are aimed at.**

Even direct mail advertisers are now able to target potential consumers for the type of products they are selling. This is despite the fact that the only information they have to go on is a list of names and addresses which they have either bought (there are hundreds of different lists on sale) or got from the register of electors which is available to anyone in local libraries. A system called 'Monica' developed by the market analysis company CACI draws inferences about people's ages from their names. For example:

Pre-family (18–25):
Lynn, Julie, Lorraine, Michell, Sharon, Kevin, Gary, Steven, Hugh, Daniel
Young family (25–44):
Pamela, Judith, Heather, Hazel, Janet, Keith, Christopher, Brian, Martin
Mature family (45–65):
Joyce, Eileen, Kathleen, Sylvia, Brenda, Eric, Frank, Dennis, Kenneth, Raymond
Retired:
Hilda, Florence, Annie, Violet, Ethel, Ernest, Percy, Herbert, Arthur, Cyril

Socio-economic status can be determined from the address. Britain's postcodes have been divided into eleven groups. These include, for example, group B; modern family housing/higher income (eg, Tamworth, Andover) and group G; poorest council estates (eg, inner Liverpool and Glasgow).

An advertiser wishing to sell, say long winter holidays in Spain, would be well-advised to direct this mail-shot at Violet and Arthur in Prestatyn (group K; better-off retirement areas). If it's nappies, then Pam and Phil in Telford or Basildon (group E; better-off council estates) are a good bet. For these people the adverts dropping through the door may not just be 'junk-mail' but actually of interest to them.

Cinema advertising has also become specialised, its target group being the unmarried young. Attendance is dominated by the fifteen to twenty-four age group, those between twenty-five and thirty-four do still go but the over thirty-fives rarely attend. It has renewed its usefulness for advertisers by redefining its audience. An additional attraction for advertisers is the possibility of creating attractive and inventive advertisements for the big screen. A screen sometimes forty-seven feet wide with amplified and high quality sound and an attentive young audience sitting in the dark is an advertising agency's dream. Furthermore, while TV advertisements are laden with restrictions, about the only thing a cinema advert can't do is incite unrest or violence among the audience. Cinema has been helped in this by the new targeting strategy of many advertising agencies. Guinness, for example, used to use 'buckshot' advertising (including women's press, national and local papers etc), but now defines its target groups as home drinkers and regular pub-goers. Gordon's gin have deliberately used cinema advertising in order to change the age profile of its drinkers. Barry Smith, creative director of Foote, Cone and Belding, formerly Gordon's ad agency says . . . 'We want young people to think about drinking gin rather than relegating it to something their parents would indulge in'.

☐ **If you are working in a group, test whether these ideas are correct. Establish whether their names give a clue to age, as suggested here. Consider older and younger relatives in addition to those present. Identify any addresses locally which give a clear indication of the socio-economic status of the inhabitants.**

Additionally, the type of film being shown allows advertisers to have a fairly clear idea about the profile of the audience. Films for the younger age group will, of course, attract bigger audiences. *A Passage to India* attained a total audience of about 2 million people in 1985, but *Ghostbusters* achieved $8\frac{1}{2}$ million. For those companies wishing to advertise gin, jeans, a new make of car or the services that their bank can offer young people, cinema is the ideal medium. Increasingly pressure groups are becoming aware of the attractions of targeting. The TUC commissioned a film encouraging a boycott of South African goods to be shown on cinema screens, while Index on Censorship, a group against restrictions on expression, also commissioned Saatchi and Saatchi to produce a three minute film about them and their cause.

2. The impact of advertising on the mass media

Views on this can be summarised under three headings.

The no-impact model

This suggests that advertising has no impact on the other sorts of content of the mass media. Those in official or establishment positions in the media tend to argue that advertising has no effect on its nature or content. For example, Stephen Murphy, a TV officer at the IBA with long experience as a BBC producer, categorically stated in an interview with media sociologist James Curran that that advertising pressure is not transferred to programme content. Similarly, Royal Commissions on the Press (1949, 1962 and 1977) have each said that it is difficult to find evidence of any such effect.

The manipulative model

This suggests that advertisers use their position of influence to manipulate the editorial content of the mass media. The page proofs of The Glasgow Media Group's *Bad News* contained allegations of subtle and crude financial pressure, but this was retracted for fear of libel action. Where a medium is largely funded through advertising revenue 'there is a pervading fear that valuable advertising will drain away in the face of persistent criticism that names and condemns specific products' (Ian Breach, the former motoring correspondent of *The Guardian*).

Perhaps the best example of manipulation by advertisers of media content comes from an examination of the rise of the 'soap opera'. Soap operas are so called because they began from an advertising campaign for soap powder. They began on American radio through sponsorship by soap-powder manufacturers, Proctor and Gamble, who made Oxydol washing powder. Proctor and Gamble were under serious competition from Unilever the makers of Rinso, but Proctor and Gamble managed to recover their market position through subsidising the radio serial *Ma Perkins*. The plugs they got in both the script and the advertisements which interspersed the story gave rise to a dramatic increase in sales of Oxydol which finally triumphed over Rinso. A modern equivalent is the manipulation of the content of TV programmes by advertisers in *programme-length commercials*. At the moment these are confined to children's animated adventure programmes. Examples include Tonka's *Go-Bots*, Hasbro Bradley's *Transformers*, *My Little Pony* (and others), Mattel's *He-Man and*

Masters of the Universe and *She-Ra Princess of Power*, and LJN's *Thunder Cats.* In total there are sixty-five series designed to sell children the characters and their apparatus. In each case the toy companies retain control over the content of the programme. The companies have found that this increases sales dramatically. Hasbro's sales literature says to retailers; 'Every GI Joe figure, every vehicle, every accessory will star in this historic television first! Think of the enormous excitement this series will generate among kids for all GI Joe toys. Get ready for the sales impact!' This sort of programme, being popular with children, is displacing other forms of broadcast children's entertainment and in virtually every case contains doubtful sex role models, attitudes towards violence, and so on.

An example from the press involves *The Observer* newspaper. Its city correspondent advised shareholders of Harrods on the best way to beat off an unwelcome bid from Tiny Rowland's Lonrho. This was in the context of a general campaign by that paper against his aggressive bid for Harrods and a more longstanding series of articles which were critical of Lonrho's dealings in Africa, particularly sanctions-busting deals with Rhodesia. Lonrho responded by cancelling its advertising in *The Observer.* Soon afterwards Rowland bought the paper. This has meant that certain areas of business and foreign reporting were subsequently not covered by the paper (eg. the paper's diarist Peter Hillmore was dissuaded from writing about Tiny Rowland's friend Conservative MP Edward Du Cann (now Managing Director of Lonrho)).

Another example of manipulation is the giving or withholding of co-operation by the military when films needing such co-operation are made. These films are beneficial because they attract recruits and improve the image of the armed forces. In a sense they are 'advertising' the armed services. The US Navy has a Hollywood liaison office which has worked with Hollywood on such films as *PT109* (about the life of John F. Kennedy), many John Wayne movies, *Operation Petticoat* and, more recently *Top Gun.* The military are the only people who own the hardware needed in such films (jets, helicopters and so on) and they loan them to 'appropriate' films. Co-producer of *Top Gun*, Don Simpson, says that the military top brass at the Pentagon were 'very positive' about his film and admits that 'we did them well'. On the other hand, Oliver Stone's *Platoon* did not get such co-operation. The military judged this film (about Vietnam) to be 'wholly unrealistic', especially in its portrayal of drug use, black–white relations and the treatment of the Vietnamese. While no-one says that the military have editorial control, they clearly only support films they consider to portray them 'accurately' (eg. *Top Gun*) and their project officer on site can withdraw co-operation at any time if anything deviates from what had been agreed.

However, arguments against the manipulative view are that:

- Commercial TV companies have a monopoly over televised advertising, hence they can resist pressure

- The IBA is vigilant about influence such as this. Loss of licence to broadcast may result

- Radio advertising time is bought in chunks. Times of transmission are set by the stations themselves on a rotation basis. This helps avoid pressure from advertisers

☐ **Examine the 'feature' pages (ie, ones about holidays, motoring, cooking, etc,) of local and national newspapers over the next week. Pay particular attention to the advertisements on the page.**

Comment on the relationship between the feature and the advertisements.
Identify which of the two above models are verified, if either of them are, by your research.

- *The Sunday Times* continued to get adverts from Distillers even when it was campaigning against that company's heartless treatment of the victims of its drug Thalidomide. This shows that a good cause, especially one with news value, will hold sway over financial pressure.

The revenue allocation model

This is more sophisticated than the last. Its main proponent is J. Curran. His argument essentially says that where advertisers place revenue in the media will affect those media in important ways, including which survive and which do not. Let's examine his argument point by point . . .

- Recent changes in where advertisers have placed their business have tended to favour the development of the regional press and have undermined the national press to some extent.

Table 6.2: Proportion of press advertising revenue derived from advertising in 1979

National Dailies	National Sundays	Regional Dailies and Sundays	Local Weeklies	Total Newspapers
44%	44%	66%	85%	59%
		high level of support here (£246 m. more than national press in 1979.)	now threatened by free distribution sheets (FDS). LWs heavily reliant on advertising revenue. If this goes to FDS then LWs will disappear. Advertising revenue of FDS 1968 = £1m, 1979 = £52m.	

Other Trade and Professional journals	Total Periodicals	Periodicals
64%	47%	54%
this high level of support has helped to sustain otherwise non-viable titles (in terms of circulation). This has led to the rise of specialist magazines.		

Source: Department of Industry, 1979, Newspapers and Periodicals. *Business Moniter* (PQ485) 4th Quarter, HMSO, London, page 312, J. Curran

Table 6.3:   Distribution of advertising revenue between the media

	1938 %	1948 %	1954 %	1960 %	1965 %	1970 %	1975 %	1979 %	1985 %
National newspapers	25	14	17	20	20	20	17	16	17
Regional newspapers	27	31	31	21	24	26	29	28	23
Magazines and periodicals	15	13	19	12	11	9	8	9	6
Trade and technical journals	12	16	13	10	9	10	9	10	8
Other publications	2	1	1	1	1	2	2	3	5
Press production costs	5	8	6	5	4	6	5	6	6
Total press	85	83	88	7	70	72	70	70	65
Television	–	–	–	22	24	23	24	22	31
Poster and Transport	8	14	9	5	4	4	4	4	4
Cinema	3	4	3	2	1	1	1	1	1
Radio	3	–	1	–	1	–	1	2	2

Identify those sectors of the press which are most financially vulnerable according to this table.

Describe and explain the trends shown in this table.

● As we have already seen, some sections of the media have had to specialise in terms of their audience in order to deliver a particular type person to advertisers. This has allowed them to continue to attract revenue in the face of competition from TV.

☐ **Illustrate this last point by giving examples of how the TV audience might differ at different times of the day and week.**

Money for *television* advertising comes from particular types of product manufacturer—household cleansing products, toothpaste, food and drink and the like. This is because TV cannot deliver a targeted audience to advertisers. Some limited selectivity is possible; the audience changes a little according to time of day and day of the week, but hardly at all by type of programme, according to Curran.

The press has managed to defend itself from competition from other media partially through its ability to deliver to advertisers a particular type of readership target group. Additionally, government limitations on broadcasting have increased the attractiveness of the Press for advertisers (though this may change if the BBC is allowed to advertise). Target marketing has led to the launch of many new periodicals, many of which check first with advertising agencies to ensure that they will reach a suitable audience (this occurred before the launch of *Over 21*, for example).

● Where advertising money is being spent has had a number of consequences for different media.

Advertising revenue allocations have reinforced the conservative bias of national newspapers. Those which can attract an affluent, middle class (and, therefore, conservative) readership can easily attract advertising revenue. Some areas of the press have disappeared altogether as a result of this. Examples include *The Daily Sketch*, *Reynolds News*, *Picture Post*, *Illustrated*, and *Everybody's.* These all closed down because they could not attract advertising income, appealing as they did to old and poor people—not an attractive proposition for advertisers. Also their circulations tended to decline as they lost readers, in particular, to the new TV medium (that group of people read less and watch more TV than others).

Conservative papers which include 'serious' news coverage can reach readers who have money to spend, have influence over corporate spending and watch comparatively little TV. Advertisers find it worth paying to get the attention of such people. For these reasons the quality papers are able to survive even with remarkably low circulations. Popular papers cannot because of their lower advertising revenue. *The Daily Herald* closed in 1964 with a larger circulation than *The Times* and *The FT*. *Women's Weekly* (read by a working class readership) derived 5p per copy from advertising revenue in 1976, *Harper's and Queen's* got 92p.

Table 6.4: Sources of revenue of newspapers

Type of publication	% from advertising 1986	% from sales 1986
Popular dailies (The Sun)	27	73
Popular Sundays (Sunday Mirror)	31	69
Quality dailies (Guardian)	58	42
Quality Sundays (Observer)	66	34
Regional dailies (Yorkshire Post)	61	39
Regional weeklies	84	16
Consumer magazines	41.5	58.5

☐ **Identify the types of magazines which will find it easiest to attract advertising revenue, giving examples.**

Political papers, in particular radical ones, do not suit advertisers. They don't have a suitable editorial environment, they don't cover a consumer market (ie, the politically committed tend not to be concerned with consumer goods) and they don't reach a specialised group. Hence, there are few of them.

Also the direction of advertising revenue allocations has caused women's magazines to be oriented to young middle class women, because such women have spare cash. Magazines for the middle class also appeal to advertisers because they use coated paper, have an editorial style that suits glossy adverts, have a high readership per copy and have a readership with a low exposure to the TV. There are $5\frac{1}{2}$ million young middle class people in the population, (young = under 35) 16 million older working class people, yet, there are far more magazines for the former category than for the latter. General women's weeklies have suffered in particular. In 1958 there were seven with a circulation of over $1\frac{1}{2}$ million each, by 1967 there were only four. They have largely been replaced by magazines for young middle class working women. Between 1965 and 1975 there were thirty-four new beauty/fashion/home interest/young woman magazines launched (compared to only seven general women's magazines launched).

Finally advertising money has added weight to private rather than public broadcasting, giving it a better financial base. Advertisers are willing to pay for a stable, reliable and predictable audience. This pushes TV programming into such populist areas as soap operas, situation comedies and variety programmes. These have universal appeal and they tend to displace more serious documentaries, current affairs programmes and the like. The BBC has been forced to adopt a populist approach, too, by the competition from the ITV stations. In 1958 the BBC's audience share dropped below 30 per cent and from that point it began consciously to imitate its rival. This policy has proved successful. In 1987 the audience share of the BBC channels overall was 48 per cent, while 52 per cent went to the IBA channels and Channel 4. Increases in the licence fee are difficult to justify if the station is not providing what the audience wants.

● The content of the media has been adapted to suit the requirements of the advertisers, Curran argues. This has had several results.

The popular and quality press have polarised, so the journalism is now very different in each. The quality press have not provided material to cater to popular tastes for fear of diluting the quality of their audience (and, hence, their attractiveness to advertisers). The popular press, though, want quantity rather than quality and, hence, they are happy to provide whatever will attract the largest number of readers; page 3 girls, scandals about soap opera stars and so on. Some advertisers will clearly be unhappy about their company name being associated with such an environment. The Co-op and Tesco withdrew their advertisements from the *Star* in 1987 because they felt that it had gone too far down market under the editorship of Michael Gabbert (Gabbert was sacked soon afterwards).

Programming on TV has been affected as channels seek to deliver a large and predictable audience to advertisers. Scheduling strategies are used to manipulate audience numbers. One is to transmit light entertainment programmes early in the evening, following them with a sequence of programmes that expand and consolidate the mass audience. Another is 'hammocking' programmes of low audience appeal between two 'bankers' (programmes which can be relied on to attract a large audience). A third is to schedule a programme of limited appeal at the same time as an equally unpopular programme on the other main channel. These are all adopted to get and keep as big an audience as possible. In commercial radio the attempt to deliver a target audience to advertisers has led to programmes for the specialist market such as *Hullaballoo*, a programme for teenagers on Capital Radio which generates appropriate advertisements (and, hence, revenue). In this way radio is trying to fight back against the loss of audience to TV.

Lastly consumer magazines have subordinated themselves to the needs of advertisers so that editorials become merely extensions of the advertisements ('aditorials'). Service features on investment, travel, motoring, property and fashion have grown in terms of editorial space in national newspapers since the war. This has been done in order to attract associated advertising revenue. Fear of loss of advertising revenue serves as a check to criticism of particular products or brands. However, the influence of advertisers is much more pervasive on women's magazines than on national newspapers. In these and other consumer magazines there is less commitment to journalistic integrity. Providing a conducive editorial environment for adverts in these magazines is much more important than it is in the national press. In some cases advertisers are invited to share the cost of editorial features (the magazine *Honey* did this on several occasions in 1973). Aditorials such as this are appearing on the deregulated commercial Italian TV though the audience is not informed that the company whose products are receiving such flattering attention is paying for the privilege.

☐ Examine the shelves of a local newsagent. Count the number of magazines directed to each special interest (or estimate the space). Identify which types of interests predominate and which are not represented. On the basis of the evidence you collect, comment on Curran's view that the press and other media have been shaped by the need to deliver target audiences to advertisers.

☐ **PROJECTS**

This is an interview study on the effectiveness of advertising.

1. Choose sample size and method of sampling.
2. Choose a current advertising campaign in the broadcast or printed media.
3. Compile a questionnaire to establish its effectiveness. The sorts of questions you might ask include:

   Have you seen the advertisment for **X**?
   Can you describe the advertisement?
   Do you know what sort of product **X** is?
   What did the advertisement tell you about **X**?
   Have you bought **X** since you saw the advertisement?
   If not, do you intend to buy any?
   Had you bought **X** before seeing the advertisement?

   You should, of course, elaborate on these questions.
4. Devise a way of collating the material you have gathered so that you can summarise the findings about the effectiveness of the campaign you have chosen.
5. Conduct the study.

☐ **Semiological analysis can be applied to advertising as to any other form of media message. Study this reading of, and advertisement for, *Johnson's Baby Lotion*.**

Underneath it all you're still a Johnson's baby.

johnson's
baby
lotion

johnson+johnson

Life is hard on a grown-up skin.
That's why you need a gentle,

effective cleanser to wipe
away what the day's put on.

'The photograph shows a clear, fresh face with an open and trusting expression. She has what could be a nappy around her neck, but apart from that there is no sign of any clothes, makeup or jewellery. She is in a state of nature, of innocence before The Fall. The copy runs Underneath it all you are still a Johnson's baby. The first three words are ambiguous. They could refer to underneath makeup, underneath clothes or underneath the image that is presented to the world, partly with the aid of accessories, clothes and makeup. You are still a Johnson's baby *makes the link between the past (baby) and present (adult) use of Johnson's and puts the reader/model in the role of a child who can rely on Johnson's as their "parent", a source of permanence in a changing, demanding world. The copy around the bottle suggests that the working woman suffers pollution of her natural state as a result of her entry into the world of work. Women need Johnson's to return them to their natural baby-like state of nature by removing the detritus of life.'*

☐ **Choose an advertisement from any magazine and attempt a similar reading of it. This can be done in an unstructured way (as above) or using the following table (one example has been given for guidance):**

Sample decoding of an advertisement

Denotive codes	Connotive codes	Promises	Problems
Young woman with towel around neck and preparing to apply *Johnson's Baby Lotion* with cotton wool.	Cotton wool and white towelling = babies. Fresh skin, open expression and no makeup = innocence, happiness and naturalness.	Return to baby-hood. Youth, happiness and authenticity.	Stresses in the adult world, especially for women. Ageing, especially for women. Responsibilities.

☐ **Write to the IBA for their current *Code of Advertising Standards and Practice*. After examining it, draw up a short list of adverts which may contravene them. The IBA's address is: 70 Brompton Road, London SW3.**

☐ **ESSAY**

The Peacock Committee, (of 1986) ... argued that the BBC should have the option of privatising Radio One, Radio Two and local radio ... But Peacock went on the recommend that the BBC should not take advertisements at the present time...

(Stephen Wagg, Mass Communications: The Debate About Ownership and Control, *Social Studies Review, March 1987)*

Discuss the possible consequences of permitting BBC television and radio to carry advertisements.

Bibliography

S. Broadbent, *Spending Advertising Money*, Business Books, London, 1979

S. Chapman, *Great Expectorations: Advertising and the Tobacco Industry*, Comedia, London, 1986

K. Myers, *Understains*, Comedia, London, 1986

G. Dyer, *Advertising as Communication*, Methuen, London, 1982

T. Millum, *Images of Women: Advertising in Women's Magazines*, Chatto and Windus, London, 1975

J. Williamson, *Decoding Advertisements*, Marion Boyars, London, 1978

J. Curran, *The Impact of Advertising on the British Mass Media*, in R. Collins *et al* (eds), *Media Culture and Society*, Sage, London, 1986, pp.309–36

M. Forrester, *Everything You Always Suspected Was True About Advertising (but were too legal decent and honest to ask)*, Roger Houghton Press, 1987

Table 6.2 from The Advertising Association Students' Brief No. 6 *Facts and Figures on Advertising Expenditure*

T.R. Nevett, *Advertising in Britain*, Heinemann, London, 1982

S. Broadbent, *20 Advertising Case Histories*, Holt, Rinehart and Winston, London, 1984

T. Vestergaard and K. Schroder, *The Language of Advertising*, Blackwell, Oxford, 1985

The Observer 4 October 1987, p.53, *They Know You*, is the source of information about CACI's Monica system and the Acorn system for dividing Britain's 1.3 million postcodes into eleven groups, A to K.

Note: The answer to the table on page 72 is X = *Cosmopolitan*, Y = *Woman* and Z = *Playboy*

7 · Industry and Politics in the Media

☐ **What view of politics and politicians does the programme encourage amongst the audience?**

The media and industrial relations

Perhaps the best known studies in this field have been conducted by the Glasgow University Media Group (GMG). This group adheres to the hegemonic perspective on the media (see page 37). Their main publications to date are given on page 23.
The methods employed by the GMG in their research are summarised on pages 23–24.

The conclusions of these studies are as follows:

● The use of words used in the broadcast news is biased: 'trouble', 'radical', 'pointless strike', etc, all structure the listeners' perspective on stories.

● Stories are reported in a selective way. For example, Harold Wilson said that a strike at British Leyland was 'manifestly avoidable' and that this was the fault of workers and management. The evening news reported him as saying that only the workers were to blame.

● The *effects* of strikes are far more likely to be reported than their *causes*.

● Visual effects are also used in a biased way, for example, film of piles of rubbish and rats may be used to reinforce the verbal message of the voice-over, both concentrating on the effects of a strike, rather than its causes. Similarly film of a group of pickets round a fire outside some factory gates shouting over each other to get access to the microphone reinforces the message of anarchic and dangerous strikers.

● The *tactics* of protestors are more likely to be reported than their *views*.

● There is a *hierarchy of access to the media*, so that 'experts' and establishment figures are more likely to get their views aired than workers and ordinary people.

● There is a unitary frame of reference given in the news, that of the dominant ideology. News is reported in a simplified and one-sided way.

● The media *set the agenda* for public debate, that is, they determine which are the most important issues of the day. This is done on the basis of the frame of reference of the reporters, which is predominantly anti-union, pro-establishment and middle of the road politically. For example, at the top of the media's agenda during the miners' strike was picket-line violence (caused by

☐ **For many of the exercises in this chapter you will need to study as many TV news broadcasts on all four channels as possible. Try to record them for later detailed analysis. If recording facilities are not available then make detailed notes while watching.**

miners). Police violence and intimidation were very much on the miners' agenda, but these were consistently absent in news coverage. Such structured absences are a consistent part of news reporting.

- In setting the agenda they act as *gatekeepers*, excluding some stories from the news and including others. Some themes will often recur in the news, for example, stories about strikes at British Leyland are more likely to be included than more important and longer strikes elsewhere and they are likely to be constructed in terms of the problems of a radical, irresponsible and greedy workforce in that company.

In *More Bad News* the GMG say that the fundamental reason for these biases is the particular world view that journalists have. This echoes the interests and attitudes of the dominant class in society very largely. The effects of this world view are two-fold:

- it defines what counts as 'news' and whose opinions are important enough to be sought, who should be interviewed and so on when telling us about it.

- it provides journalists with a way of interpreting events and 'explaining' them.

They, therefore, subscribe to the hegemonic model of media bias we discussed in chapter two. In their more recent *War and Peace News* they seem to have added some elements of the manipulative theory to their analysis of media bias. For example, they stress the pressures on broadcasting journalists to put the establishment line, even if it does not accord with their own view. Sometimes, however, journalists can 'escape' these pressures and present a critical point of view or even an anti-establishment line. Jonathan Dimbleby is named specifically as a TV journalist whose views are out of the ordinary for a journalist and has been able to use the media to express them. Powerful forces within and outside the media have an important influence on journalists, but they don't totally control them.

☐ **Make a note of any examples you find in the news broadcasts you study to illustrate these findings.**

EWS OUTSIDE BROADCAST

AMERA TWO, CLOSE UP ON THE BLOOD, CUT TO FLYING ETS, CAMERA FOUR, DISGUSTED STRIKERS' WIVES. CUT TERVIEW WITH CHIEF CONSTABLE, ROLL THE MENTARY, "HOW MUCH MORE CAN PUBLIC STAND?"....

☐ **An interesting assignment to test the statements made by the GMG and others about the world view of journalists is to interview a journalist or journalists. It will be most convenient, probably, to approach a journalist on a local paper near to you. Journalists often begin their career on local papers and progress to nationals or to the broadcast media anyway. In advance of the meeting prepare a detailed list of questions. These should be designed to assess such issues as whether s/he feels s/he has total freedom in the way reports are written, particularly reports of strikes etc., what the main constraints on news reporting are, what makes a 'good story' and so on. Delicate areas such as the journalist's political views and attitude towards unions will have to be approached with some caution.**

Criticisms of the Glasgow Group's work

A well-researched and cogent critique of the work of the GMG has recently been written by Professor Martin Harrison of Keele University. Harrison was allowed access to the transcripts of the ITN broadcasts and most of his comments relate to their news coverage, not that of the BBC (though he believes that they are probably true of the BBC as well). Using this and other information he makes the following criticisms of the GMG's findings:

- The five months which the *Bad News* study covered was not representative in terms of the pattern of industrial relations in the country (there were an abnormally large number of days lost in strikes) or of news behaviour (which at different times of the year would have adopted other stories, for example, during the conference season).

- The GMG were selective what they looked for (eg, they claimed that there was no news reporting of employers' lock-outs, withholding pay or refusing overtime money, in fact there were several instances of such reporting).

- The GMG are mistaken in believing that undue attention is given to strikes in some industries (eg, car manufacture, especially at British Leyland), while other industries are ignored (eg, shipbuilding). In fact, news values are determined at least as much by the 'knock on' effects of strikes beyond the plants actually involved as by the measure of the number of days lost. Also, the official statistics by which the GMG measure the 'real' severity of strikes are crude and inaccurate at best.

- The GMG argue that the media are too concerned to illustrate the effects of strikes on consumers of goods and services. However, it is legitimate to give priority to the effects rather than the causes of strikes when those affected outnumber strikers by more than one thousand to one in some cases.

- The GMG have a naive view of news values; priority is often given to stories which have a historical background (for example years of strikes at British Leyland). This background is lost by the short term nature of content analysis studies and is not appreciated by the GMG. Novelty, too, is important in news values, as are stories which involve broader issues (eg, a strike over the introduction of containers at London docks involves the question of new technology versus jobs). Strikes with a political dimension and those which for some other reason are controversial are also likely to be reported. How many competing stories there are on a particular day will also be an important determinant of whether a strike story is, or is not, included. To sum up, news values neither work consistently for the trade unions nor against them. Film may be chosen because it is good visual material, not for any anti-union message it may contain.

- A number of the allegations made by the GMG about TV news are simply not true. Harrison demonstrates this by reference to statistical material from the ITN transcripts. These unfounded allegations are:
  - that the news does not normally name the trade union involved in a dispute.
  - that the news does not normally state whether a dispute is official or not.

- that the news does not normally state the cause of an industrial dispute.
- that access is not normally given to shop floor workers in unofficial disputes.

For example, the ITN report of a strike by Glasgow's dustcart drivers stated who was on strike, mentioned the TGWU, the application for the strike to be made official and the essence of the men's demands.

- The GMG's approach, while claiming to be objective and scientific, is actually slanted in favour of the unions and searches for only one sort of bias. While there is a chapter entitled *The Trade Unions and the Media* in *Bad News* there is no chapter on *Management and the Media.* This needs to be studied too, as management also argues that the media are biased against them (the management organisation Aims of Industry claims that most managers believe this). It is harder to persuade management to appear on TV than unions, argues Harrison. Consequently, broadcasters have to put management's side of a dispute for them. Indeed, in a sample of television news coverage of the first eight months of the coal dispute it was found that the time given to pro-strike miners, their families and NUM officials outstripped that given to the NCB (eighty-nine minutes compared to thirty-five minutes and 30 seconds). It was only when the NCB realised that their low profile was having this effect that this imbalance was corrected.

- The GMG make sweeping generalisations on the basis of very sparse examples and evidence. For example, they found two cases (out of 216 studied) where a worker had his /her occupation or position captioned in lower case letters, for example, 'shop steward' rather than 'SHOP STEWARD'. On this evidence they include a ten page section headed *'Lower Case is Lower Class'.*

- On the specific point about Wilson's speech, the main thrust of the speech was against the workforce at British Leyland in general and the Cowley plant in particular (which had been strike prone for some years). Though the management's deficiencies were also mentioned, this was a side issue. Certainly the press interpreted the speech in this way:

WILSON ISSUES ULTIMATUM TO CAR STRIKERS

MR WILSON WARNS WORKERS THAT STATE WILL NOT BAIL OUT STRIKE-HIT FIRMS

Harrison's basic argument is that there are numerous pressures on the media, many of which are in competition with each other:

'Television is more productively considered not as essentially one-dimensional but as conveying a range of contradictory contentions and explanations—the site of ideological conflict, rather than simply fostering "a climate of conformity".' (p.127)

The GMG have picked up on one of the elements in television and presented this as the only one, usually on the basis of limited and selective evidence. Their selection has been guided by their own

□ **On the basis of your analysis of TV news, which side appears to be correct; Harrison or the GMG?**

ideological position and commitment, one which is quite firmly on the left.

Greg Philo, speaking for the GMG, replies that Harrison undertook the book on the suggestion of, and partly financed by, ITN. This has undermined his academic impartiality. More importantly, the transcripts used by Harrison and supplied by ITN are inaccurate. '... sections of the text broadcast by ITN are missing. Some are very long ... Most are smaller ... There are dozens of transcription errors ... plus, astonishingly, the inclusion of passages which ITN did not in fact broadcast.' Philo implies that Harrison has been duped by ITN, who supplied him with poor evidence in order to sustain their case. He concludes that Harrison 'has produced a study of television content without having either the pictures that were shown or the actual words that were spoken' and as such his book cannot be regarded as a serious critique.

However, most practising journalists would agree with Harrison's point that the broadcast news is the site of a battle between conflicting views and interests. They see themselves simply as acting as the conduit for a variety of views. For example, Nicholas Jones, Labour correspondent of BBC radio news, argues that radio news is itself neutral. Any bias in industrial reporting is due to the differing ability to communicate which workers and management have. Industrial disputes are increasingly about getting publicity, with each side trying to win approval for their stand in the hope that this will help them to win their case. Jones quotes the use of *The Jimmy Young Programme* as a kind of tennis ball in a rail dispute, with Sir Peter Parker (then chairman of BR) and Ray Buckton (of ASLEF) appearing on alternate programmes to reply to each other. In the coal dispute of 1984–5 the NUM eventually lost the propaganda battle for and through the media, not because of any bias in the media but because they relied too heavily on the presentational skills of Arthur Scargill. This led to a disjointed portrayal of their side of the dispute rather than one based on a proper communications strategy. While successful in the short-term, reliance on Scargill alone could not be sustained throughout a long-running dispute. The NCB won the advantage in using the media to present its case in the final few weeks. In this they were building on the techniques of news manipulation developed by British Rail, British Steel and particularly by Sir Michael Edwardes when he was chairman of British Leyland. One of his techniques was to give press statements from behind the steering wheel of his car so that he could simply drive away from any embarrassing questioning. His management team carefully monitored news reports so that any 'inaccuracies' could be 'corrected' by phone. Jones admits that BL's methods led journalists occasionally to feel themselves under pressure to reflect management's interpretation of 'the facts'.

□ **Politicians and pressure groups manipulate news in the same way. For example politicians insert catchy phrases ('the loony left', etc) into speeches in the hope that they will be picked up by reporters and journalists. Pressure groups use famous people or pull stunts in order to get into the news. Over the next few days note examples of tactics used to get into the headlines and onto broadcast news.**

Unions, on the other hand, are only just becoming adept at media manipulation. They suffer the disadvantage that there are often a number of them involved in one dispute, so it is difficult to ensure that 'the union view' is presented clearly and consistently to the media. Many unionists have an inbuilt suspicion of journalists and so refuse to talk to them. Despite this there have been attempts, especially by the TUC, to use the media as effectively as management do. The Labour Party, too, has become media-conscious, following the trail blazed by the Tories in this respect.

There are, however, a number of problems with Jones' answer to criticisms of studies like that of the GMG, which he states is one of the reasons why he wrote the book. Perhaps the main one is that he is only referring to *radio* news. It is true that on radio there is more time to hear a variety of views on an issue. Both unions and management are often given the opportubity to air their views on the news and, more especially, on the numerous programmes given over to current affairs by Radio 4. Moreover, the medium lends itself to giving a fuller background to a dispute than television news does. So, while there might be a case for the idea that the radio presentation of industrial disputes is neutral, television presentation is not. Constraints of time, the nature of the medium (being primarily visual rather than oral) and the quite different nature of programming all mean that the charges levelled by the GMG still stand. Furthermore, one can sense in Jones' book an antipathy towards Arthur Scargill and what he stands for. Meanwhile, moderate trade union leaders like Scargill's predecessor Joe (now Lord) Gormley get approval. There is even a sneaking admiration for management, despite their clever ploys for manipulating journalists like him. This, if true, confirms the GMG (*et al*) view about the unitary and essentially conservative world view of middle class, male, white journalists like Nicholas Jones.

☐ **Listen each day this week to the *Today* programme on Radio 4 (transmission times usually 6.30 am to 8.40 am weekdays). In-depth coverage of the sort referred to by Jones is provided here, often with contributions from Jones himself. Does the evidence from the programmes tend to confirm or refute Jones' view?**

Politics

The press and politics

Because the press is not hampered by the necessity to remain neutral on political issues it is easier to find evidence of bias here than in broadcasting. This is especially the case in the tabloid (popular) press. Critics of the press put their case as follows:

The majority of national newspapers are pro-Conservative. In the 1987 general election the following twelve papers supported the Conservative Party: *The Daily Mail, The Mail on Sunday, The Sun, The News of the World, The Daily Telegraph, The Sunday Telegraph, The Times, The Sunday Times, The Sunday Express, The Star, The Daily Express, The Financial Times.* These had a combined circulation in the region of 22 million copies.

The following four papers supported the Labour Party: *The Mirror, The Sunday Mirror, The Guardian, News on Sunday.* Their combined circulation was around 7 million.

Today and *The Independent* supported the Alliance. Their circulation amounted to less than 1 million.

Newspapers, thus, do not represent the views of the electorate. Only 42 per cent of those who voted cast their vote for the Conservatives in that election. The majority opted for some other party (Labour polled 30 per cent and the Alliance 22 per cent). Many people did not bother to vote at all.

Newspapers do not confine their political bias to the editorial pages They allow it to enter their presentation of the 'news' so that the truth becomes distorted. Examples of this are many and some recent notorious ones are:

The hounding of the homosexual Labour Party candidate Peter Tatchell in the Bermondsey by-election:

RED PETE WENT TO GAY OLYMPICS (The Sun)

(Tatchell did *not* go to these olympics, held in San Francisco)
The Daily Mail's claim that if Labour were to be elected in 1983 Nissan would not build its car plant in this country, at a cost of 35,000 new jobs. (This claim was denied by Nissan itself.)
The persecution of the peace movement and the Greenham Common women:

CND HOLDING HANDS WITH IRA—POLICE ANGER AS DEMOS TAKE MEN OFF BOMB WATCH DUTY
(The Standard 20 December 1983, three days after the bombing of Harrods)

The quote is from an unnamed police officer and the intention of the headline is clearly to link the CND with the bomb outrages, a ludicrous suggestion.

CHAOS AT MARCH AS SEVENTEEN HELD (The Sunday Express)

This related to a CND rally of 200,000 people in London. The 17 were arrested on minor charges which hardly merited the word 'Chaos'.

CND: IS IT ALL A RUSSIAN CON TRICK?
MOSCOW MAKING FOOLS OF OUR BAN THE BOMB BRIGADE.
(The Sun)

This followed a trip to Moscow by representatives of the Northern Friends of Peace Board, an offshoot of the Quaker movement and headed by a peer and a Roman Catholic priest. No journalist has ever managed to confirm these allegations of Soviet manipulation of the peace movement which crop up from time to time.

MOBBED: HESELTINE IS FLOORED
(The Sun)

TARZAN'S WAR: HESELTINE FELLED BY WOMEN
(The Daily Mirror)

JEERING PROTESTORS PUNCH MINISTER
(The Times)

ANGRY PEACE GIRLS ROUGH UP HESELTINE
(The Sun)

This story relates to an event which took place in Newbury (near Greenham Common) in February 1983 when Heseltine was Minister of Defence. While the police were rushing him through a hostile crowd he tripped and fell to the ground. He was unhurt. The Ministry of Defence confirms this, stating that he was not pulled to the ground by anyone.

Nonetheless, according to the newspapers the peace women were punching him, dragging him to the ground, kicking him and spitting on him.

The vilification of Tony Benn is another example. Shortly before the Chesterfield by-election in which he successfully stood as the Labour Party candidate *The Sun* ran a story headed:

BENN ON THE COUCH

Supposedly based on psychoanalysis of Benn by a psychiatrist, the story ran ... 'Some say Tony Benn is raving bonkers. But what really goes on in the complex mind of the country's most notorious left-winger? ... He is greedy for power and will do anything to satisfy his hunger ... Tony Benn is a man driven by his own self-interest and thinks of himself as God.'

In fact the psychiatrist, Dr Hubbard, had been telephoned in America by *The Sun* and given a summary of Benn's main characteristics as seen by the journalists. He admitted not spending much time on the assignment and not knowing that it concerned a prominent British politician.

Critics of the press presentation of politics would also point out that there is very little in the way of real politics reporting in the tabloids besides this sort of sensationalised story involving conflict between the good guys and the bad guys (and, in Greenham Common, women). In a sense this very omission is a political act, they argue. The popular press take people's minds off the serious issues of the day by giving them trivial rubbish to think about. The aim is to keep them uninformed and, therefore, politically placid. Examples are legion. Journalists devote a lot of time and attention to 'Sudsology' as they call it (ie, stories about soap operas and their characters):

I'M STAYING IN THE STREET SAYS LEN (*The Mirror*)

DEIRDRE AND MIKE LEFT DANCING IN THE DARK (*The Times*)

This last story was about the extra-marital love affair between two *Coronation Street* characters. Experts were consulted by *The Mirror* and horoscopes prepared for Deirdre and Mike, despite the completely fictional nature of the whole issue. More recently attention has shifted from *Coronation Street* to *EastEnders*, with Dirty Den replacing Hilda Ogden in the affections, or otherwise, of tabloid journalism.

Generally stories which are exciting and unusual will get into the papers, they need not be true (or even rational):

UFO LANDS IN SUFFOLK—AND THAT'S OFFICIAL
(*The News of the World*)

A story based on very little evidence and bearing a remarkable and suspicious resemblance to events in the film *Close Encounters of the Third Kind* appeared in *The Sun*:

IS YOUR NEIGHBOUR FROM OUTER SPACE? (*The Sun*)

Apparently the way to tell is by the following signs:

If you are studying the media in a group, buy copies of all the daily newspapers on one particular day and allocate them among the different members of the group. In half an hour or so each member should:

- identify particular examples of bias in one direction or the other with regard to industry or politics (attention should be given to editorials and cartoons, as well as news stories)
- roughly quantify the amount of attention given to stories about these two issues compared to other types of news (foreign, crime etc)
- prepare a summary of what the main news values of that particular paper are, perhaps in order of priority (eg sport, foreign news, domestic political news, sudsology etc)

Individual reports can then be given to the group as a whole and comparisons made.

- Aliens sleep and work unusual hours (the day on their native planet is different from ours)
- They show anxiety, stress or discomfort when using earth transportation
- They read a lot of newspapers and magazines to get as much information about earth as possible
- They own unusually large amounts of high tech equipment
- They misuse everyday equipment such as food mixers and vacuum cleaners
- They have homes with ill-matching decorative schemes
- They have an unusual object in the home which is highly regarded and protected and 'could be from the alien's planet and used for communication'

With the exception of the third, these signs would suggest that *Sun* readers are themselves inter-planetary visitors!

Sex, of course, is a constant theme in the tabloids. This is dealt with in more detail in another chapter. Suffice it to mention here that sex is used even in 'political' stories, thus once again diverting attention from the real issues:

WOMEN WHO VOTE SDP AND LIBERAL ARE RED-HOT IN BED
(*The Sun*)

GREENHAM IS A LESBIAN COMMUNITY—FOUR OUT OF FIVE ARE LESBIANS (*The Sun*)

Needless to say, the tabloids are more interested in the sex lives of ministers and ex-ministers such as Jeffrey Archer and Cecil Parkinson than in their policies.

In the broadsheet press there is a particular form of bias in political reporting which is subtly introduced. It results from the lobby correspondent system. Lobby correspondents are privileged journalists who are allowed to watch and record debates in Parliament and have access to parts of the building where others are not allowed to go. MPs give them privileged information and they get special press briefings from the Prime Minister's press secretary and from Government departments. They get advance copies of documents and they can usually get answers to questions they wish to put to members of the Government. The *quid pro quo* for all this, though, is that they must work according to the Lobby Rules: 'The cardinal rule of the Lobby is never to identify its informant without specific permission . . .' and '*DON'T TALK ABOUT LOBBY MEETINGS BEFORE OR AFTER THEY ARE HELD*'.

Peter Hennessy (formerly *The Financial Times* Lobby correspondent) argues that this secrecy and privilege means that Lobby correspondents are used by the Government to manipulate the news. Unofficial 'leaks' with no attributable source can be given to the Lobby correspondents in order to shape public attitudes. Lobby correspondents know that they must not give offence to the authorities or they will lose their privileges and the easy access they have to news stories. Hennessy is not alone in this critique of the Lobby system. This system means that the Lobby correspondents give up any independence they once had as journalists and become, in effect, the mouthpiece of the Government. They take their line from the official view and allow the timing of the release of news to be dictated by the Government and the civil service.

The broadcast media and politics

The broadcast media, unlike the press, have an obligation to remain politically impartial. Some authors argue, though, that they are not. Again, the Glasgow Media Group are prominent among them. For *Really Bad News* they studied news coverage of the Labour Party in much the same way as they examined coverage of industrial relations. They found that the right wing of the Labour Party and the 'wet' face of Toryism get particularly sympathetic coverage. Extremism, either on the right or on the left, is given the same sort of treatment that striking or immoderate unions get.

The GMG's finding that TV news is biased in favour of the political middle ground is supported by a much earlier study conducted by Blumler and McQuail called *Television in Politics: Its Uses and Influence.* Interviewing a panel of respondents on three occasions before, during and after the election campaign of 1964, they found that the effect of Party Political Broadcasts was mainly to shift opinion in favour of the Liberal Party. More interesting though, was the finding that television news coverage was even more influential than the Party Political Broadcasts in shifting opinion in this direction. The reason why this is so, according to Blumler and McQuail, is quite different from that suggested by the GMG. Blumler and McQuail argue that TV can reach uncommitted voters (who would not bother to attend party rallies etc) and that they will naturally tend to support middle-of-the-road policies. The pro-liberal influence of the media is therefore a result of the nature of the audience, and not any bias in the media institutions themselves, as the GMG believe.

Here are two studies with complementary results (though different explanations of them). One focuses on media output, the other on the effect the media have on the audience. As the broadcast media seem to prefer the centre ground of politics it comes as no surprise that the SDP achieved public prominence as soon as it was set up in 1981, though its subsequent showing in the polls and later merger with the Liberals suggests that this was mainly media hype rather than founded on real public support.

A variant of the hegemonic theory (see page 37), argues that the media frequently initiate a moral panic about 'the state of society today' (because of blacks, the unions, youth or whatever) and in so-doing establish the basis for the legitimate installation of repressive measures by the authorities. This is the basic argument of *Policing the Crisis.* The authors of the book maintain that the capitalist economy goes through periods of crisis from time to time. The profitability of companies declines, many go out of business. There is unemployment and hence increased poverty. Inflation rises and there are currency crises. Levels of discontent increase. At such times the capitalist establishment needs to keep a tight grip on society. The powers of the forces of law and order need to be strengthened and trade unions and political dissidents are intimidated into quiescence. However, this cannot be done by using the brute force of the police and army in a simple and direct way. To do so would unmask the basic brutality and oppressiveness of capitalism. First the approval of the public for such measures must be obtained. This is achieved by the media's whipping up of concern about 'the collapse of law and order'. The climate is soon right for increasing police powers, political arrests, harsh sentences and so on.

An example of this process in action is the year-long moral panic about 'mugging' in 1972. This was followed by a tightening of what they call the 'control culture', that is, the police and courts began to act with increasing vigour against deviants. Similar moral panics can be identified prior to this, for example, the 'cosh boy menace' (1951), teddy boys (1954), soccer hooligans (periodically from 1961), mods and rockers (1964), skinheads and hell's angels (1969).

In a similar vein, Steve Chibnall's *Law and Order News* argues that crime reporting is used to reinforce consent for the dominant ideology in capitalism. He suggests that law and order news during the period 1965–75 was organised around the dominant theme of 'The Violent Society'. There was a single over-riding image; that of a law and order crisis. This arose as a result of:

- the pro-capitalist ideology of most of the media (concerned about any erosion of the stable social base for the profitable exploitation of the working class),

- the news values of journalists which are highly compatible with this ideology (looking for stories which arouse the emotions, which involve goodies and baddies etc) and the fact that the dominant source of news stories was the forces of law and order themselves, particularly the police. Their interpretations of events were accepted uncritically and, if they needed to, they could manipulate the media to their own ends.

The same theme is found in Liz Curtis' *Ireland: The Propaganda War*. She argues that the army in Northern Ireland is the most trusted supplier of news to the media institutions. The media allow them regularly to lie and use their privileged access for their own propaganda ends, and to cover up torture, brutality and mistakes. Moreover, programmes are routinely censored by broadcasting and publishing media so that the views of the Catholic republicans are not allowed expression. A blind eye is turned to Protestant loyalists' violence while that of the IRA is graphically described and portrayed as motiveless. People killed by soldiers 'die in an incident involving the army'; those killed by the IRA are 'gunned down by terrorists'. In this way the consent of the bulk of the British people is built up and maintained for the Government's policy in Northern Ireland. From a Republican point of view, of course, that policy involves the maintenance of an army of occupation by a colonial power.

One of the main problems with any examination of political bias in the media is that, even where it can be shown to exist, it is very difficult to demonstrate that it has any effect on the audience. The insights provided by the 'uses and gratifications' approach should make us wary of the dangers of simply assuming that bias in the media is automatically translated into attitudinal changes among the audience (in other words, of implicitly accepting the hypodermic model of media influence).

☐ **Proposals for harsher legislation followed media hysteria about child sex abuse cases in Cleveland in the Summer of 1987. Are there any more recent examples you can find?**

Attitudes one holds prior to exposure to the media will strongly influence one's response to any bias. Thus, if the news about Northern Ireland is pro-Unionist it will receive only derision from Northern Ireland Catholics. Similarly pro-Conservative messages will simply be ignored, rejected or refuted by strong Labour supporters. This suggests that those with strong political opinions will be unaffected by political bias in the media, or will merely have their ideas confirmed through the processes of selective exposure, selective perception and selective retention. Students of voting behaviour such as Ivor Crewe tell us that the British population as a whole are becoming increasingly less attached to particular political parties and political philosophies, and more likely to change their vote between elections. This process is known as *partisan dealignment.* This is illustrated by the fact that before 1970 about 45 per cent of the electorate strongly identified with one or other of the two major parties, but by 1983 only 22 per cent did so. With fewer people with fixed political affiliations around, the power of the media to persuade and influence is probably greater than it was twenty years ago.

☐ ESSAY

'Reporting "news" is inevitably partial, selective and biased.' Discuss with reference to the reporting on industrial relations by the media.

'Television is a means of communication, not persuasion'. (Michael Grade) Critically evaluate this statement.

☐ PROJECT

Construct a questionnaire designed to establish how far the respondents' political view influences their choice of newspaper, their perception of the political standpoint of particular papers, and of the influence of the press on their own views.

Bibliography

P. Hennessy, *What the Papers Never Said*, Portcullis Press, 1985

M. Cockerell, *et al, Sources Close to the Prime Minister*, Macmillan, London, 1984

J.G. Blumler and D. McQuail, *Television in Politics: Its Uses and Influence*, Faber and Faber, London, 1968

A. Hetherington, *News, Newspapers and TV*, Macmillan, London, 1985

N. Jones, *Strikes and the Mass Media*, Basil Blackwell, Oxford, 1986

Glasgow Media Group, *Bad News More Bad News Really Bad News War and Peace News* RKP, 1976, RKP, 1980, Writers and Readers, 1982, and Open University Press, 1985 respectively

J. Downing, *The Media Machine*, Pluto Press, London, 1980

M. Harrison, *TV News: Whose Bias?* Policy Journals, Berkshire, 1985

Philo's reply to Harrison is taken from a letter from Greg Philo to the journal of NATFHE April 1986 pp.28–9

S. Hall, *et al, Policing the Crisis*, Macmillan, London, 1978

S. Chibnall, *Law and Order News*, Tavistock, London, 1977

Liz Curtis, *Ireland: The Propaganda War*, Pluto, London, 1984

H. Porter, *Lies, Damned Lies and Some Exclusives: Fleet Street Exposed*, Chatto and Windus, London 1984. This is the source of many of the examples of newspaper stories quoted in the text.

J. Hartley, *Understanding News*, Methuen, London, 1982

P. Schlesinger, *Putting Reality Together—BBC News*, Constable, London, 1978

B. Whitaker, *News Ltd—Why You Can't Read All About It*, Comedia, London, 1981

Minority Press Group, *Here is the Other News*, Minority Press Group, London, 1980

8 · Women and the Media

Most of the work about women and the media has been written from a feminist position. In this chapter we will;

1. Examine some of the criticisms made by feminists of the media's portrayal of women and review some of the evidence they have presented.

2. Explore the reasons for any biased treatment of women.

3. Examine the effects of this bias.

1. Feminist criticisms of the media treatment of women

The media portray women in only a limited number of roles; the nagging wife, the difficult mother-in-law, the sex object, and so on. Women are rarely pictured as combining a marriage and successful career. Where women *are* seen as strong and dynamic, they are usually both single and sexy;

> '*Wonderwoman was incapable of doing her amazing tricks unless she shed all her clothes except a one-piece that exhibited starkly her full figure. The continuing message of* The Incredible Hulk *seemed to be that beneath the feyest male lurks massive power, even if his clothes-shedding somehow seemed to split his shirt but not his pants.'* (J. Downing, The Media Machine)

Strong and dynamic women can also be quite stupid in the mass media:

> '*Supergirl, a being of strength approximate to that of Superman himself and thus able to push planets out of orbit without working up a sweat would spend her time either frolicking with Supercat or Superhorse, or maybe falling in love with the young men from the bottle city of Kandor who would always turn out to be villains who wanted to use her in order to revenge themselves of Superman.*
> * Somehow she never realised this until it was too late, no matter how many times it happened, not even when all her Kandorian boyfriends had names like E-Vill and Nars-Tee and the like.' (A. Moore,* Sexism in Comics)

Men, of course, are portrayed in a wider number of roles and in a much more positive light.

Women are, thus, seen in a very limited, one dimensional way. This is most apparent in pornography, which treats them as flesh rather than human beings. While porn may be considered a minority taste, this is becoming less true with the spread of VCRs. It is estimated that altogether Americans watch between sixteen and 20 million pornographic video films per week and that even the higher social classes are beginning to watch them.

TV advertisements in particular treat women in a stereotyped way. One study of women in TV advertisements found that:

- women were seven times more likely to appear in ads for personal hygiene products than not to appear

- 75 per cent of all ads using females were for products for use in the kitchen or bathroom

- 38 per cent of females in ads were pictured inside the home, compared to 14 per cent of males

- men were significantly more likely to be shown out of doors or in business settings than women

- twice as many women were shown with children than were men

- 56 per cent of women in ads were judged to be (only) housewives

- forty-three different occupations were coded for men, eighteen for women.

Related to this point is the argument that women's bodies are exploited quite unscrupulously in advertisements as sexual commodities to sell anything from after shave to motor cycles.

An interesting content analysis study of the presentation of women in soap operas comes from D.M. Meehan's, *Ladies of the Evening: Women Characters of PrimeTime TV.* The methodology she employs is described on page 24. She suggests that there are essentially only ten female character types presented in the American drama serials she studied. These are:

1. *The Imp*: a rebellious tomboy character. She is adventurous, not really sexual, often finds herself in trouble. The imp is the opposite of what society expects a woman to be and the trouble she gets into is often a result of this (eg, Elly Mae Clampett in *the Beverly Hillbillies* and Sabrina in *Charlie's Angels*)

2. *The Goodwife*: is domestic, attractive, home-centred and content. She does not wish to become involved with the world outside the home, leaving this to her lucky husband (eg, Olivia Walton in *The Waltons*)

3. *The Harpy*: is an aggressive single woman. She is powerful, even overpowering, and not afraid to take on or chase after men (eg, Hot Lips Houlihan in *MASH*)

4. *The Bitch*: is a sneak and a cheat. She is manipulative, dangerous and deceitful. She lacks the power to be a real villain (invariably male), but she causes real trouble for the forces of good (eg, Sable Colby in *The Colbys*)

5. *The Victim*: is the passive female who suffers accident, disease or violence, depending on the type of show. Medical series, in particular, very often have female victims of disease, especially if the doctor is young and handsome (eg, *Young Doctors*)

6. *The Decoy*: is a heroine disguised as a victim. Apparently helpless and dependent, she is actually strong and resourceful. She is quite likely to be mistreated, hurt or captured, but she is capable of

☐ **Try illustrating these characters by reference to more modern serials you are familiar with.**

☐ **Watch an episode of any current American drama serial on television. Pay careful attention to the female characters in it. Do they conform to one or more of the ten character types described above? Are there any character types in the episode which fall outside these. If so how would you describe that type? If you are working in a group, take one serial each for analysis. Later, present your findings to the group as a whole for discussion.**

In your view, does the characterisation of women in British serials differ significantly from the types outlined in Meehan's study of American serials?

☐ **Another example of 'The Witch'**—*I Dream of Jeannie* **(American Comedy programme). Attempt a semiological reading of this photo. See page 80 for an example to help you.**

☐ **Studies of women in the media very often discuss the sorts of roles they are portrayed in, as Meehan does here. However there is rarely any analysis of male roles.**

Make a list of the soap operas currently on BBC and commercial television. Then note down the important *male* characters in them. Finally classify them into 'role types' in the same way as has been done above for women.

☐ **These figures are fairly easy to test using content analysis (see page 23). Why not try it? You could compare different soaps to identify those which are more and less sexist in the number of women they portray.**

overcoming her difficulties. Often she is the physical and intellectual superior of many of the men in the show (eg, Purdy in *The New Avengers* and Jennifer Hart in *Hart to Hart*).

7. *The Siren*: The Siren of Greek mythology was a female creature who lured sailors to their deaths with her tantalising voice. The TV siren is equally dangerous, using her sexuality to lure her victim to a sticky end. This female character often appeared in Western series such as *Maverick, Bonanza* etc.

8. *The Courtesan*: is close to being a prostitute, and perhaps is or has been one (this information is not for American television audiences, however). In Western series she appears as a saloon keeper or cabaret hostess.

9. *The Witch*: has extraordinary power deriving either from a supernatural source or from extreme wealth. Despite this the witch is invariably dominated by a man and is persuaded, often reluctantly, to suppress her power or use it for his aims. Samantha in *Bewitched* is perhaps the best example. She uses her limitless power mainly for domestic tasks and to help her rather stupid husband, Darrin, in his advertising career.

10. *The Matriarch*: has power, prestige and authority. She is seen in a positive light, despite the fact that she is too old to be sexually attractive. Her status is almost that of a hero. As a result of all this she is a character rarely seen on American drama serials, (eg, Granny Moses in *The Beverly Hillbillies* and Ma in *Bonanza*).

Other findings of this study are:

● That women are portrayed as either good or evil, never a combination.

● That 'good' women are portrayed as submissive, sensitive and domesticated.

● That 'bad' women are portrayed as rebellious, independent and selfish.

● That male evil characters are always counterbalanced by good ones. This is not so with female evil characters.

● That the number of occupations which women are portrayed as holding is limited to a few, primarily housewife, receptionist and whore. Male roles are also few in number compared to reality but are more exciting; doctor, spy, detective, astronaut etc.

● That women are portrayed as lacking any sexual appetite (with the notable and recent exception of Jennifer Hart in *Hart to Hart*).

The *number* of women portrayed in the media, especially on TV, is much smaller than the number of men. The exact figure depends on the medium being discussed, but a general figure of half as many women as men on TV is often quoted. Soap operas have a relatively high proportion of women, though they are still outnumbered by as much as seven men to three women depending on the type of soap opera. Cartoons have a particularly low number of women (often stylised as cats, etc). In advertisements there are three all-male ads to every one all-female ad.

Related to this point is the view that women are made less visible than men in a different sense; through the sexist use of language on television. Most textile workers are women, yet their product is known as 'man-made fibre'. Forty two per cent of the workforce is female, yet they are said to contribute 'manpower' to the economy (when they are discussed at all). The media have only to use the English language in a normal way and women disappear.

Men of all ages, attractive or unattractive, are to be seen in the media. Women generally will be under thirty and physically attractive. This is even true in women's magazines where the women are generally young and thin. There is a powerful ideology of contentment and domestic bliss as well as an escapist concentration on the life of the stars in these magazines.

Sex role stereotypes are confirmed and supported in more subtle ways than just the portrayal of roles. Commercials for girls' products have soft and melodious music, those for boys have loud and dramatic music. About 97 per cent of voice-overs (the authoritative voice with an unseen face in adverts) are male voices, often instructing women about how to use washing powder or similar items. Other figures of authority (weathermen, newsreaders) are usually male, though sometimes with a token, and very attractive, female. Especially for young viewers, this leads to the expectation that women need to be attractive if they are to be in a position of authority and that the normal holders of such positions are men.

News values, (that is, what is considered news-worthy) are male in orientation. Women's issues are treated frivolously. For example, the famous bra-burning by womens libbers never happened; it was an invention of the press. Women's sports are rarely featured on television and in the press. The special problems women face are either ignored or trivialised. Women's Lib is treated in terms of the loss of femininity which is thought to occur to its supporters. Stories involving women stress their physical appearance ('*Brunette stabbed to death*' was the headline of the American *Daily News*, with underneath in lower case letters *6,000 killed in Iranian earthquake*).

Rape is treated in an evocative way, and given so much over-reporting that the public generally overestimate the level of sexual crimes in society. The official statistics record sexual offences as only 0.6 per cent of all recorded crime in 1985 (though this is probably an underestimate—there are between four and ten times as many rapes committed as there are reported) yet they figure much more largely than this in most newspaper crime reporting. The victim of rape attacks is viewed, it is claimed, with almost as much hostility as the aggressor in many of these reports.

Big stars of the cinema are virtually all men nowadays (though for the earlier generation there were numerous big female stars such as Marilyn Monroe, Bette Davis, Lauren Bacall, Mae West and Katherine Hepburn).

'Women's media' are of a quite different type from others. Women's pages in daily newspapers deal with soft news, the family, fashion and other material which is considered too trivial for the general media. Advertisements figure very highly, indeed such pages could be seen as merely a vehicle for advertising. Budgets are very low for them, and there seems now to be a certain amount of embarrassment about their

□ **Study the advertisements on commercial TV for the next few days. Note any examples which confirm or refute this criticism of them.**

□ **Watch the next edition of *Sportsnight*. How many women appear in it? Do your findings suggest to you that any action needs to be taken?**

□ **List the first ten film stars you can think of. How many of them are women?**

nature. *The Observer* has a supplement called *Weekend* which is clearly designed to be for women. Other papers, too, feel it necessary to find some euphemism for 'women's page', normally something like *Living*. Radio Four, though, has no such qualms. Its afternoon programme is called '*Woman's Hour*'. Presumably, the rest are all 'Men's hours', despite the fact that the Radio 4 audience on a weekday is predominantly female.

A detailed study of women's magazines was conducted by Marjorie Ferguson and published in *Forever Feminine: Women's Magazines and the Cult of Femininity*. As a woman, a journalist of ten years' experience and a PhD student of Sociology she was particularly well-qualified to study the treatment of women in women's magazines. She conducted a content analysis study of the three largest-selling women's magazines:

Woman
Woman's Own and
Woman's Weekly.

In this she concentrated on only some parts of their content:

Features (which cover many subjects, including the life of the stars, real life drama etc)
The Problem Page
Beauty
Fiction

Two studies were made, the first taking a random sample of issues for the period 1949–74. The second took issues between 1979 and 1980 to see what, if any, changes had occurred in the 1970s. In addition, she interviewed thirty-four women's magazine editors about their role, beliefs and professional practices. Additionally, ninety-seven journalists, artists, publishers and managers were interviewed about their perceptions of the editorial processes, publishing organisations and market context of women's periodical production.

The dominant themes identified by the content analysis of the magazines of 1979–80 are summarised in the table below.

Table 8.1: Dominant themes, all subjects[a], all titles, 1979–80 (%)

Order		W	WO	WW	Total

Order		W	WO	WW	Total
1	Self-help: overcoming misfortune	35	32	40	36
2	Getting and keeping your man	11	10	15	12
3	Self-help: achieving perfection	13	14	6	11
4	The happy family	9	12	12	11
5	Heart versus head	12	8	12	10
6	The working wife is a good wife	9	13	7	10
7	Success equals happiness	11	8	8	9
8	Female state mysteries	–	–	–	–
9	Gilded youth	–	–	–	–
10	Other	–	3	–	1
	n	24	24	24	72

[a] Excluding beauty
n = 1 per item, 3 items per issue, 4 issues per year;
W = *Woman*; *WO* = *Woman's Own*; *WW* = *Woman's Weekly*

Source: M. Ferguson, *Forever Feminine*, Heinemann, 1983

☐ **Between 1949 and 1974 the relative positions of these themes were quite different. This 1979–80 'winner', self-help (overcomes misfortunes), came a poor second then (only 10 per cent of items), while the top theme then was today's number 2; it appeared in 59 per cent of items. The rest were as follows: 3rd heart versus head (9 per cent), 4th this happy family (8 per cent), 5th the working wife is a *bad* wife (3 per cent), self-help (achieving perfection) (3 per cent), female state mysteries (2 per cent), gilded youth (1 per cent), success equals happiness (1 per cent), other (3 per cent). Account for these changes.**

Her fundamental conclusion is that women's magazines convey what she calls a 'cult of femininity'. This is: '. . . a set of practices and beliefs: rites and rituals, sacrifices and ceremonies, whose periodic performance reaffirms a common femininity and a shared group membership'. These magazines instruct women in values and attitudes about being a woman. They tell women what to do and how to think about themselves, about their men, colleagues, children, neighbours and bosses. The novice is instructed in how to achieve her chosen ends: what to wear, how to act, and what to buy to be a *femme fatale*, super cook or office boss. Ferguson notes that this is unique among women's magazines; magazines for men do not instruct them in 'how to be a man'. It is assumed that men know everything there is to know about being masculine. Moreover, though the *content* of the instruction has changed over the years (see table), the instructional nature of women's magazines has not changed.

She may be wrong, though, in her contention that there are no male equivalents of women's magazines. There appears to be a new breed of 'men's magazines' which do not cater for a specific interest and are different from the old-style men's magazines like *Mayfair* and *Fiesta*. Examples include *Om* (Options for Men), *Unique*, *Arena* and *Q*, despite the scepticism of observers who point to the failure of similar ventures in the past (who now remembers *London Gentleman*, or *Sportsweek*?). *Arena* tends to concentrate on fashion, *Q* on music, *Om* on both as well as other traditionally male concerns. They tend to sell between forty and sixty thousand copies each. Their rationale is that, with the increasing segmentalisation of advertising, there is now room for 'men's magazines' of this type.

2. The causes of the distorted representation of women in the media

Feminists are agreed that there is a distorted portrayal of women in the media. There is, however, a certain amount of debate among them on the reasons for this. We can simplify the different perspectives on this and other issues concerning women under the following headings:

Liberal feminism
Radical feminism
Socialist feminism

Liberal feminism

Liberal feminists argue that individuals are trained by the mass media and other social institutions into patterns of behaviour which are performed unconsciously. Sex roles, in particular, have been built-up over a long period of time and have become embedded in our culture. They can, however, be changed by a conscious process of rooting out those elements in society which perpetuate them. Clearly the media are one of the most important targets in this process.

Journalists have learned to portray the female world in a particular way; as classless and home-and-family based. They can easily un-learn this and begin to portray women differently. Indeed, this process has already begun, some feminists argue. The old stereotypes of women belonging to one of two types: *Waiting to Wed* and *Wife and Mother*

have now been joined by a third; *Independent Woman.* A new breed of magazines has grown up for working women which deal with far wider issues than just home and man.

Recent TV series have moved away from the old machismo approach and recognise the emancipation of women in a way which is both realistic and unafraid. Women in positive and non-sexist roles include Elaine Nardo in *Taxi,* Joyce Davenport in *Hill Street Blues,* and the two American policewomen in *Cagney and Lacey.*

Despite this, there is much to be done. Media images of women change only slowly in response to real social changes. This 'culture lag' is due to the fact that ideas and attitudes change more slowly than material conditions. Women are still ignored and trivialised in much of the media and so their symbolic annihilation continues. However, we can expect a slow change in this as the media catch up and increasingly reflect the new social position of women. Tuchman in *Hearth and Home,* for one, believes that this is increasingly the case. The liberal feminist position, then, is quite close to the pluralist one—they both believe that the media largely reflect public attitudes and social realities.

Radical feminism

Radical feminists identify men as the enemy. They believe that men consciously and unconsciously manipulate social institutions for their own benefit and to the detriment of women. The family is a crucial site of this oppression, but the media are in the hands of men too, and are an important weapon against women.

Men hold the dominant positions throughout the media and are able to use them to reflect the images of women which they desire. A study conducted for Thames TV in 1977, for example, showed that there were nineteen male presenters or commentators for every one woman. A 1981 survey of the same company showed that not one of the fifty-four upper management jobs was held by a woman. The media consist of the powerful talking to the less powerful and men talking to women. The issues which affect women, such as discrimination at work and in education, sexual harassment, the problems of baby care, social isolation, attitudes of the police in rape cases and so on are not dealt with, or are trivialised. This male-centred perspective is demonstrated by the press treatment of a small advertisement placed by a Vietnamese woman during the Vietnam war. She offered to marry any man who could take her away from the war. The story was dealt with not in terms of the suffering she must have been undergoing but the fact that she was available to *any* man.

D. Meehan argues in *Ladies of the Evening* that the Goodwife image, in particular, represents a male yearning for a time when the family was a woman's central concern. The popularity of programmes in which the Goodwife appears is due to men's fear of the women's movement and the increasing competition women are offering in the job market. The domesticity and submissiveness of the Witch was attractive for similar reasons. However, some of these characters appealed to women as well as men, the Imp because of her rejection of the boring domestic role, the Witch because of her implicit power over men. Generally, though, most American series express men's fear of women, particularly in the modern world. This is obvious in the machismo series such as *Shaft, Cannon, The Rifleman* and so on, whose very titles contain symbols of the penis ('phallic symbols') and which include few, if any, central women characters. The radical feminist position, then, echoes the manipulative theory we examined in chapter two. Here, though, it is men who are manipulating both the content of the media and women's attitudes.

Socialist feminism

Socialist feminists blame capitalism as an economic structure for the disadvantaged position of women in society. Women give their labour cheaply. They serve as a reserve army of workers who can be called on when the need arises and then sent back into the home. They are also useful to the capitalist class for breeding purposes; they bring the next generation of workers into the world. In addition, they help to sustain and pacify the male workers by providing a comfortable home, meals and sexual services for them. Finally, they are super-exploited by capitalism as consumers and as sex objects.

The role of the media in all this is to sustain and perpetuate the capitalist system and the supporting role of women in it. Big business effectively controls editorial content of women's magazines in particular. That women are portrayed in traditional ways is in the interests of the capitalist class: it justifies using women as a reserve labour force ('send them back to the kitchen when not required in the factory') and paying them lower wages ('the pretty things can't earn a real wage').

The pattern of ownership of the women's press would seem to lend some weight to this argument. Four companies effectively control the production of women's magazines in this country:

- IPC: *Woman's Weekly, Woman's Own, Woman, Woman's Journal, Woman's World, Ideal Home* and *Honey*

- D.C. Thompson: *My Weekly, The People's Friend* and *Annabel*

- Standbrook Publications: *Family Circle* and *Living*

- National Magazine Company: *Cosmopolitan, Company* and *She*

   (IPC is owned by Reed International. Only D.C. Thomson is independent of a multinational conglomerate).

However, crude capitalist manipulation of the media is not considered particularly important by most socialist feminists. What the media are doing is articulating the male-centred ideology of capitalism in an unconscious way. Editors, even female ones, interpret the wider world in terms of the 'woman's angle'; a trivial and home-centred one. Anything else (for example, the Greenham Common women) gets little attention and, when it does appear, is treated dismissively or critically. There is a clear opposition between the women's movement and the mass media. The women's movement defines the woman's position positively, the media define it negatively (ultimately around the concept of 'finding a male'). While it is true that 'Independent Woman' has become a feature of women's magazines recently, this is really only a new version of earlier stereotypes. 'Independent Woman' is expected eventually to become 'Wife and Mother'. The implication is that her career is only a temporary phase of her life. The dominant theme of women's magazines between 1949 and 1974 (getting and keeping your man) has been replaced by self-help instructions for the working woman. The message of 'get out there and win' has 'remember you also achieve as a wife and mother' added to it. This, then, is a variant on the hegemonic perspective we examined earlier. The dominant ideas and values reflected in the media are those of the men who control its content.

The pluralists' response

Pluralists argue that if the media portrayal of women and the content of women's magazines is skewed in a particular direction, this is only what the audience require. The specialist groups involved in media production merely cater to public demand. A *Women's Weekly* editor interviewed by M. Ferguson said:

> *A lot of features actually come from readers letters. The whole business about 'too scared to make love' was readers' letters. They were all still writing in about how, when, if—you know, all that sort of thing. I thought, 'Blimey, so a lot of them are doing it and don't know how to, and are scared stiff'.*

There followed a frank series of articles about sex and sexual relationships. For the editor, then, this was not a propagation of any 'cult of femininity', merely a response to public demand.

Editors judge their success by total sales, advertising revenue and overall profitability. Presumably, the best way to achieve these is to appeal to the tastes of the market they cater to. The most successful media, on these criteria, are also the most traditional in terms of their attitudes towards women. Magazines which stick to the traditional format (*Good Housekeeping*, *Women's Weekly*) tend to thrive. Those which attempt to be more modern like *Nova* (which was stillborn) and *Spare Rib* (the women's movement magazine) do not. This is because women are still quite traditional in their views and interests.

The pluralist argues that increasingly there are new periodicals for women. Many of them adopt a different stance from the traditional ones and do not espouse the 'cult of femininity' or at least are preaching a different version of it. A variety of messages will be available for women, some rejecting the 'cult of femininity' entirely. Pluralists would also argue that the media are trendsetters. Women are presented equally, with female newscasters, journalists and producers being the rule rather than the exception nowadays. Studies show that viewers find women in such roles just as authoritative as men.

As far as advertisements are concerned, those portraying non-traditional roles are far more common than they were. David Lipsey, in an article in *New Society*, argues that sexist advertisements on TV are now the exception rather than the rule thanks to the work of the women's movement, women's greater spending power and changes in public attitudes.

The pluralist believes that while the media *used* to be sexist, they no longer are. Public awareness of women's issues became so great in the seventies and early eighties that the problem no longer exists to any great extent. It is noticeable that many of the studies of sexism in the media are concerned with programmes shown in the past—even as far back as the 1950s. Attitudes among producers and writers, as well as among the audience, about what is and what is not acceptable have

☐ **Conduct a survey asking people a series of questions about newsreaders (you supply a list of names). Questions could include:**

**From this list, who is your *favourite* newsreader?
Who presents the news most convincingly?
Who do you trust most? and so on.**

Use the results to compare people's reactions to female and male presenters.

come a long way since then. This is particularly noticeable if one compares the children's books of today with those of the '50s, '60s and even '70s. The old sex role stereotypes have now been purged from their pages (as have the racial ones).

☐ **Prepare a table that will enable you to analyse advertisements for the degree of sexism in them. The following examples may help:**

Product	Voice-over (M/F)	Dominant person (M/F)	With children (M/F)
I. Corn flakes (give a brief description of the ad)	M	M	F

(You will need to think of more categories; these are just an indication.)

Watch commercial TV for as long as possible, filling in the table when the adverts appear. The aim is to test whether the pluralists are correct about the representation of women in advertisements or whether critics of it, like those quoted on page 96 are right.

☐ **Go to your local library to conduct an analysis of sexism in the young children's books available. Prior to your visit you should prepare a scheme to help orgainise your research, perhaps by listing possible sexist criteria so that points can be given, contributing to an 'index of sexism'. Make a note of the date of publication of each book so that any trends can be identified.**

● **Note the date, author and title of the book.**
● **Note the number of male and female characters in it and assess the centrality of each to the story.**

As far as the radical feminists' manipulative theory is concerned, there is very little evidence for it. Despite the potential for manipulation of content that the ownership patterns suggest, pluralists believe it has never actually occurred, apart from in the past to a *very* limited extent. Throughout the war, women's magazine editors, Government Ministers and civil servants met regularly at the offices of the Periodical Proprietors Association. The aim was to teach women the practicalities of what to do and what not to do in wartime Britain for the national interest. The only peacetime equivalent to be discovered by researchers, however, was the agreement among Cookery Editors to adopt metric measurements in their recipes to help the process of metrification! As for the media reflecting bourgeois hegemony, the dominant ideas in society, to the pluralist this means only that they give a voice to what most people feel and believe. It is nothing more or less than the duty of the media to do this.

3. The effects of the biased portrayal of women in the media

Feminists of all persuasions agree that the media have a negative effect. In general terms we can sum it up by saying that the socialisation of girls and boys becomes distorted by the media. Sex roles (defined as 'social guidelines for sex-appropriate appearance, interests, skills, behaviours and self-perceptions') are reinforced by the media portrayal of women. Girls are led to have a low self evaluation and limited ambition in life. They may grow up with a 'victim mentality', seeing themselves as helpless without a man around. Boys, particularly those with little contact with females, grow up with a very strange view of what women are like. This can have unpleasant consequences, especially for the females with whom they come into contact.

More specifically, the consequences that the media's representation of sex roles has for both men and women are as follows:

- Men's attitudes to women become limited to seeing them not as people but as representing one of a limited number of stereotypes. This is demonstrated by L. Gross and S. Jeffries-Fox who found that boys who watched a considerable amount of TV more often gave the sexist answer to the following questions (the sexist answer is in italics):

  1. True or *false*—Women have less chance than men to get the education for top jobs.
  2. *True* or false—Men are born with more drive to be ambitious and successful than women.
  3. *True* or false—By nature, women are happiest when they are making a home and caring for children.
  4. True or *false*—Our society discriminates against women.
  5. *True* or false—Women have just as much chance to get big important jobs, they just aren't interested.

- These prejudiced *attitudes* will become translated into discriminatory *behaviour*. Male employers whose attitudes towards women have been affected by the media will be disinclined to give them jobs ('their place is in the home'), promote them ('they're only interested in babies really'), give them responsibility ('too emotional'), and so on. Teachers and others in positions of power will be affected in the same way. The media are partly to blame, then, for the continued disadvantaged position of women in British society.

- Women are persuaded to accept and collude in their role. Women undergo the process of 'modelling', that is, imitating a role model seen on the TV. Frueh and McGhee interviewed children in American kindergarten and asked them about the amount of time they spent watching TV, testing the extent and direction of their sex-typing. Traditional sex role stereotyping was positively correlated with heavy viewing.

- Because of the small number of high-status female models in the media available for girls to model themselves on, the *ambitions* of real women are limited. The power of the media in this respect is thought to be very strong. This is not surprising, as the average American girl will have spent more time in front of the TV by the time she is fifteen than she will have spent in the classroom. A study conducted by Beuf (1974) was based on sixty-three interviews with boys and girls between the ages of three and six. Some girls had abandoned their ambitions even by this early age:

'Several girls mentioned [that their ambition] ... could not be realised because of their sex. One blonde moppet confided that

what she really wanted to do when she grew up was fly like a bird. 'But, I'll never do it', she sighed, 'because I'm not a boy'. Further questioning revealed that a TV cartoon character was the cause of this misconception.'

- Women suffer anxiety and stress as a result of the above, and because advertising and soap operas create concerns in women particularly about:

  their body image (which rarely lives up to those on the screen)
  the constant need to spend money on products to make them more attractive and desirable for males
  competition with other women in the fight to get and keep a man.

Additionally, domestic friction may occur when real wives and mothers cannot match the looks or performance of the women that *men* see on TV.

However, in considering the influences on the attitudes of children and others we should not forget that the media are just one among many. Parents, peer groups, brothers and sisters, teachers and others can all affect one's views, particularly in early life. If the media do have a pernicious influence it is more than possible that this can be outweighed by other social forces. It is too easy to fall into the 'hypodermic' view of the media when considering these issues. We have seen already that even children do not simply *accept* the messages of TV and other media; they have to work at making sense of them (see page 23). In doing this they bring into play attitudes that they have learned elsewhere. This is demonstrated by an experiment conducted by K. Durkin and P. Akhtar. They showed an advertisement for the perfume *Impulse* to a group of four to nine year olds. In it, the woman wearing the perfume is given flowers by a man, a complete stranger who rushes up to her on a station platform. The younger children explained the man's actions in terms of a general liking for the woman and were unaware of the supposed role of the product. However, most laughed at the suggestion that the man might give flowers to the train *driver* or that the *woman* might give flowers to the *man*. In other words, the children use their background knowledge about sex roles to interpret a particular instance of stereotyped behaviour on television.

☐ **EXERCISE**

Item A

'... everything about Jackie *is designed to capture the interests of its desired readership.* Jackie *is a modern (and, therefore, young) girl's name. It's short, snappy and up-to-date, and so offers a point of immediate identification to its potential readers. Each week's cover displays this week's* Jackie *smiling out of the picture towards the passing girl, the reader. And in so far as the model looks smart (never sloppy), pretty (never plain), and cute (never aggressive), she also sets the limits to which the reader should aspire in terms of appearance. Yet hidden behind her smile is another sign, one of complicity about who the real focus of attention is. Along with the listed contents (Will You Be His Dream Girl?), the coyness and flirtiness of the model's expression leaves the reader in no doubt. The glance is primarily aimed at the handsome "guy" who is just*

about to appear round the corner, just about to get off the next bus. In this way the cover graphically defines both its market and the consuming passions which seemingly characterise such a market....

Ostensibly Jackie, *along with the rest of the pop media, aims to entertain, to give pleasure. With magazines, this involves looking and reading, while with music obviously the emphasis is first on listening and then also on looking. But in both cases these actions are not as simple as they seem. They also imply* ways *of looking,* ways *of listening.* Jackie *teaches us* how *to look in both senses. How to find an attractive self-image is part and parcel of learning how to look at* Jackie *and its view of the world, uncritically. In other words,* Jackie *presents its readers with relatively closed sets of meanings ... Readers and listeners alike are rarely encouraged to attach any importance to relationships and friendships which are not romances. Apparently devoted to leisure and fun, their idea of fun, and especially* Jackie's, *is almost wholly restricted to the neurotic search for a 'fella'. It is in these limited self-images, and the narrow possibilities they present, that the brunt of my criticism lies ... Instead of having hobbies, instead of going fishing, learning to play a guitar, or even learning to swim or play tennis, the girl is encouraged to load all her eggs in the basket of romance and hope it pays off ... No story ever ends with two girls alone together enjoying themselves. A happy ending means a happy couple, a sad one, a single girl ... The Cathy and Claire page addresses itself to the day-to-day life of the readers ... once again what girls are advised to do corresponds to looking at the world and the women's role in a certain way. And, as far as* Jackie *is concerned this involves sticking strictly to the* status quo. *... For example if a girl has a problem with an unreliable 'fella', the advice is invariably to let him go—only because she's bound to find a more suitable partner in the near future (not because it may be more fun to be single.)' (A. McRobbie,* Just like a *Jackie* Story, *in A. McRobbie and I. McCabe,* Feminism for Girls, *Routledge and Kegan Paul, London, 1981, pp.113–29)*

Item B

'Whatever the drive is that keeps thousands of women ... buying magazines like Cosmopolitan *every month, it has more to do with improvement than entertainment. Why else should one curl up after a hard day at work with a publication that tells you to "Shape up for summer—NOW", "Tune into that TOP job", "WORK off that extra weight" and "Don't daydream, dare to SUCCEED" ... "Change your face in a day, Slip into a loose T-Shirt, Learn a language this summer" ... However urgent and immediate these exhortations may sound, the subject-matter of the articles they refer to changes very little over any stretch of time ... fundamentally they revolve around the same issues of work, sex, emotional life, and feminism ... Fulfilment, for modern woman, seems to be fixed just around the corner, always an article away, on the other side of sole giant "SHOULD".' (J. Williamson,* Miss Piggy's Guide to Life, *in J. Williamson,* Consuming Passions, *Marion Boyars, London, 1986, pp.55–63)*

1. Using evidence from items **A** and **B**, compare and contrast the role played by *Cosmopolitan* and *Jackie* in the process of sex role socialisation. (5 marks)

2. In what ways are the mass media in general involved in the process of sex role socialisation? (10 marks)

3. What criticism might be made of the argument, often put forward by feminists, that the mass media play an important role in the oppression of women in a patriarchal society? (10 marks)

☐ **PROJECT 1**

It is not only women who are subject to the sorts of distorted representations in the media listed in the first section of this chapter. Old and young people of both sexes and people in higher and lower social classes are frequently portrayed in stereotyped and often demeaning ways.

Using the first section of this chapter as a guide, prepare a written project on the media representation of *old people*. The following gives guidelines on what its contents might include (in each case you should give examples from the media to support your statements):

a) List the major roles in which old people are cast in the media (you could try giving the roles names as Meehan did for the presentation of women).
b) Differentiate between the presentation of old people in different media and genre (eg, in newspapers versus TV, in soap operas versus situation comedy).
c) Comment on news-values as far as the representation of old people is concerned.
d) Describe the provision of programmes and publications for old people in the media (you could study the monthly *Yours* which describes itself as 'the newspaper for the young at heart' and on daytime Channel Four *Years Ahead* which is described in the programme guides as 'the over–60s niche' and is presented by retired newsreader Robert Dougall)
e) Comment on any different treatment accorded by the media to *old men* as opposed to *old women* in different parts of the media.

☐ **PROJECT 2**

A more sophisticated variation on the task concerning sex role stereotypes in advertisements above is to conduct a content analysis (see page 23) on a few episodes of one particular soap opera. If you can legally video-record them in advance this would be helpful. Your aim is to quantify the representation of women in that soap. You will need to identify in advance precisely which elements of this you will be looking for. For example:

the number of women in each episode (compared to the number of men)
the amount of time they each spend on screen
what occupations the men and women have
how long they are seen in traditional roles (baby-care, in the kitchen etc) and so on.

□ ESSAY

What evidence is there of the use of stereotypes of women in the mass media and to what extent do such stereotypes influence social attitudes towards women?

The aim of the project is to test whether the criticisms made of the media portrayal of women are true of soap operas. It may be that nowadays women are often portrayed in important jobs exercising considerable power.

If you are working in a group it would be useful to conduct the same exercise on two quite different soap operas (say *Dallas* and *Coronation Street)* so that a comparison of the results can be made.

Bibliography

A. Moore, *Sexism in Comics, The Daredevils*, No 4, April 1983. Extract quoted in J. Hartley, *et al, Making Sense of the Media*, Block 1, Unit 1, page 29.

D. Lipsey, *A Black Mark For Advertisers*, New Society, 21 August 1987, pages 11–13

L. Busby, *Sex Role Research in the Mass Media*, Journal of Communications, 25 (4); pp. 107–31.

M. Mattelart, *Women, Media, Crisis: Feminists and Disorder*, Comedia, London, 1986

R. Dyer, *The Dumb Blonde Stereotype*, BFI, London, 1973

M. Ferguson, *Forever Feminine: Women's Magazines and the Cult of Femininity*, Heinemann, London, 1983

D.M. Meehan, *Ladies of the Evening*, Scarecrow Press, New York, 1983

K. Durkin, *Television, Sex Roles and Children*, Open University Press, Milton Keynes, 1985

H. Butcher, *et al, Images of Women in the Media*, Birmingham, 1974

G. Tuchman, *et al,* (eds) *Hearth and Home: Images of Women in the Mass Media*, Oxford University Press, NY, 1978. This is the source of the figures on the number of women in TV serials and the information on the studies of Frueh and McGhee and by Beuf, including the quote from the latter (page 36)

L. Gross and S. Jeffries-Fox, *What Do You Want To Be When You Grow Up, Little Girl?*, in G. Tuchman, *Hearth and Home, op cit* pp. 240–71. See table 14.4 for figures on sexist response to the five questions discussed here

J.R. Dominick and G.E. Rauch, *The image of women in network TV commercials*, Journal of Broadcasting, 16 (3); 259–65, 1972. This is the source of the set of figures on women in TV advertisements (page 96)

J. Downing, *The Media Machine*, Pluto, London, 1980

M. Ferguson, *Imagery and Ideology: The cover photographs of traditional women's magazines*, in Tuchman, *et al, op cit*

C. Cockburn and L. Loach, *In Whose Image?*, in J. Curran, *et al, Bending Reality*, Pluto, London, 1986, page 15

K. Durkin and P. Akhtar, *Television, Sex Roles and Children*, New Society, 7 April, 1983

A. Hoffman, *Revelation for the Hell of it*, Dial Press, New York, 1968

B. Gunter, *Television and Sex Role Stereotyping*, 1986

D. Bouchier, *The Feminist Challenge*, Macmillan, London, 1983. This is the source of the three-fold classification of feminism. A more complex categorisation is given by M. Maynard in *Current Trends in Feminist Theory*, Social Studies Review, Vol. 2, No. 3, January 1987. She distinguishes between: Marxist Feminism; Feminist Marxism; Freudian Feminism; Materialist Feminism and Radical Feminism.

'A tip ? Who do you think I am, Social Security ?'

This chapter follows the same broad structure as that on women and the media. The issues will be examined in this way:

1. The media's representation of racial minorities
2. The reasons for this bias
3. The effects of any biased treatment of these groups

The media's representation of racial minorities

The media show coloured people in stereotyped roles, just as they do women. The following lists some of those stereotypes:

● *Parasites:* who have come to Britain just to live off the social security system:

WE WANT MORE MONEY, SAY THE £600 A WEEK ASIANS

(*The Daily Mail*, 5 May 1976—this was their reply to the question 'do you want more money', and is not a surprising one as they were actually getting £46 per week for a large family from the DHSS, the £600 referred to being the cost of their accommodation).

MIGRANTS 'HERE JUST FOR THE WELFARE HANDOUTS'
(*The Daily Telegraph*, 5 May 1976)

□ **Which areas of music and sport are (and are not) thought to be the province of black musicians and sportsmen/women? What are the reasons for the segmentalisation of sport in this way?**

● *Athletes and musicians:* this is the only positive stereotype, but the context is limited to these occupations, and indeed to particular parts of them. Blacks are supposed to be good at only certain sports and particular types of music.

- *Criminals:* West Indians, in particular, are portrayed as either criminals already or potential criminals, especially prone to street crimes such as mugging.

> *BLACK CRIME: THE ALARMING FIGURES*
> violence double that by whites, Yard reveals
> (*The Daily Mail*, 11 March 1982)

- *Sambo types*: happy, laughing, dancing imbeciles with rolling eyes and widespread empty grins. This stereotype is more or less dead now. In early films, though, it was the dominant image of the black person. The earlier 'talkies' picked up the image and it reappeared time and time again. Examples include Al Jolson, blacked up with burnt cork for *The Jazz Singer*, reincarnated in TV's *Black and White Minstrel Show*, now defunct, happily. *Gone With the Wind* had its fair share of racial stereotypes, including this one, and the less acceptable black would-be rapists and liers. In older films, too, the 'Uncle Tom' character often appeared. This one is old and wise and completely contented with the system which has whites in the dominant positions of society. The female version of this happy slave image is the 'Mammie'; a very fat domestic servant, usually with a scarf wrapped around the head. A version of this stereotype makes an occasional appearance in *Tom and Jerry* cartoons, usually on a chair trying to avoid Jerry.

☐ **The Minstrel Show** – a children's television programme of 1954, four years before **The Black and White Minstrel Show. In your opinion, was it suitable children's viewing?**

- *Brute savages:* more likely to boil a missionary in a pot and eat him than take up Christianity. This is a model particularly prevalent in children's adventure stories, at least in the past.

- *Pidgin English speakers*: people who are capable of speaking only a caricature of English and whose own language is so incapable of expression that they prefer to speak pidgin English whenever possible. Examples of this are easy to find: in Westerns the Indians used the 'Whiteman Speak With Forked Tongue' mode of expression, while in sit-coms like *Mind Your Language* much of the '*humour*' of the programme was based around this point.

- The main interest of the media concerns the *numbers* of black people coming into Britain and the threat increasing numbers pose to the jobs and facilities available to the white population.
  '. . . in Brent white families are outnumbered three to one by blacks' (BBC Documentary *Race: The Way We Live Now*)

> *ASIAN FLOOD SWAMPS AIRPORT*
> (*The Express*)

> *3,000 ASIANS FLOOD BRITAIN*
> (*The Sun*)

> *PAKISTANI SMUGGLING PLOT*
> (*The Daily Express*)

> *2,000 INDIANS SMUGGLED IN*
> (*The Daily Express*)

Black people in Britain are almost invariably treated as being in a conflict situation, with the police, with whites or amongst themselves.

BATTLE OF BRIXTON
100 black youths in clash with cops
(*The Sun* 11 April 1981).

Almost invariably it is the black groups themselves who are blamed for causing the conflict, just as miners are blamed for violence with the police. For example, *The Observer* has the front page headline following the Brixton riots:

THE NIGHT BRIXTON BURNED

But on page 3 is a story headed

SOUTHALL RIOT POLICE ARE CLEARED

'it is virtually certain that no action is to be taken against any police officers after nearly thirty complaints about police behaviour during the Southall disturbances two years ago'.

Table 9.1: British press coverage in four newspapers, in column inches, by topic and by newspaper, 1963–70

Topic	The Times		Guardian		Daily Express		Daily Mirror		All papers	
Housing	74	(6)	82	(10)	29	(5)	54	(8)	239	(29)
Education	74	(9)	121	(15)	47	(5)	4	(1)	246	(30)
Health	108	(7)	18	(4)	0	(0)	19	(1)	145	(12)
Employment	75	(4)	80	(10)	24	(3)	27	(3)	206	(20)
Numbers	84	(10)	59	(5)	9	(3)	23	(4)	175	(22)
White Hostility	100	(8)	140	(14)	99	(7)	136	(9)	475	(38)
Black Hostility	50	(4)	63	(4)	46	(5)	71	(7)	230	(21)
Discrimination	86	(7)	345	(32)	33	(4)	106	(13)	570	(56)
Discrimination by Coloureds	0	(0)	37	(2)	0	(0)	0	(0)	37	(2)
Police	72	(7)	83	(8)	34	(3)	52	(5)	241	(23)
Racial Harmony	0	(0)	17	(3)	72	(1)	8	(1)	97	(5)
Crime	213	(25)	125	(18)	358	(19)	218	(17)	914	(79)
Disturbance	16	(2)	116	(5)	32	(1)	0	(0)	164	(8)
Normal	150	(21)	107	(11)	275	(14)	258	(16)	790	(62)
Cultural Differences	46	(5)	122	(10)	79	(5)	21	(3)	268	(23)
Celebrities	4	(1)	8	(1)	100	(6)	139	(7)	251	(15)
Immigration	691	(51)	754	(76)	382	(20)	228	(18)	2,055	(165)
Legislation	284	(26)	213	(19)	76	(6)	11	(1)	584	(52)
Race Relations	493	(44)	738	(75)	327	(24)	189	(20)	1,747	(163)
Sport	27	(2)	5	(1)	15	(1)	0	(0)	47	(4)
South Africa	39	(2)	0	(0)	2	(1)	0	(0)	41	(3)
Rhodesia	72	(1)	0	(0)	33	(2)	0	(0)	105	(3)
Other	82	(10)	92	(10)	157	(12)	220	(11)	551	(43)
TOTAL	2,840	(252)	3,325	(333)	2,229	(147)	1,784	(146)	10,178	(878)

☐ **What do these figures show about:**
(a) the news values of the press in general and the reporting of race issues
(b) the different news values of the four papers identified?

What methodological problems are there with this sort of content analysis study?

Notes: Figures in brackets refer to number of items.

Source: OU Mass Communication and Society, DE 353, Block 5, Unit 14, *How the Media Reports Race*, p. 9 © (1977) The Open University Press.

☐ **Study the tabloid press for one week. Note any items which confirm or refute these statements.**

This sort of one-sided portrayal is one of the reasons for the *News on Sunday*'s editorial charter's statement that the paper:

> '*will express its commitment to anti-racism and anti-sexism both in its employment practices and in its news and features coverage. It will reflect the multi-cultural composition of British society.*'

● British media coverage of the Third World is both limited and stereotyped. The limitations of the reporting may be summed up as:

THE COUP–WAR–FAMINE SYNDROME

In other words, we hear very little of Third World countries unless there is some sort of trouble. As a result, we acquire the impression that nothing else ever happens there. It appears that the government and people of these countries are somehow inadequate because they cannot solve these problems. Such countries are pictured as having an ever-extended begging bowl held out to the rich countries.

Idi Amin, Uganda's former president, was the subject of a wide range of racial stereotypes. Initially he was the pro-British good guy;

> '*General Amin will be good for Britian. He is a big, bluff, popular man whom everyone knows as "Idi" (pronounced Eady).*
> (Tom Stacey in *The Daily Express*, 26 January, 1971)

GOOD LUCK GENERAL AMIN
'*I wish him the best of British luck*'

(Ian Colvin in *The Telegraph*, 17 February, 1971)

However, by the following year Amin had become first a fool (in the 'laughing Sambo' mould) and then a madman:

THE WILD MAN OF UGANDA
(*The News of the World*, 24 September, 1972)

HE'S NUTS
(*The Sunday Mirror*, 12 September, 1972)

In later years, Amin came to be seen as a cannabalistic tyrant, keeping enemies in the freezer for later consumption and killing thousands without a thought. This is a common 'Third World Dictator' stereotype, ex-Emperor Bokassa being another example.

Even white foreigners are subject to this sort of treatment, especially when they come into conflict with Britain. The treatment of Argentina and its people during the Falklands conflict of 1982 is a case in point:

WE'LL SMASH 'EM
(*The Sun*, 6 April, 1982)

Argentines quickly became stereotyped into Gauchos (Latin American cowboys) or simply Argies—

STICK THIS UP YOUR JUNTA!
A Sun Missile for Galtieri's Gauchos
(*The Sun*, 1 May, 1982)

PANICKY ARGIES FLEE BAREFOOT
(*The Sun*, 3 June, 1982)

Their lives were not really worth considering—

GOTCHA!
(Headline of *The Sun*, 4 May, 1982 after the sinking of the General Belgrano with nearly four hundred lives lost)

On television news the loss of Argentinian life was treated with as little gravity. Reports of the Belgrano sinking concentrated on the numbers recued, not how many had been killed. The word 'dead' was replaced by 'lost' or 'missing':
Newscaster: 'The Argentines say there were around 700 survivors from the 1,082 men on board the General Belgrano which was torpedoed on Sunday'.
Newscaster: 'The first group of survivors from the Argentine cruiser *General Belgrano* have been brought ashore. The General Belgrano was torpedoed by a British submarine on Sunday; 800 men have been rescued and the searches still continue for others'.
(ITN, 5 May, 1982 and BBC News 6, 5 May, 1982, respectively)
The sinking of *The Sheffield*, a British warship, was treated quite differently. Casualties and deaths were the main focus, and emotive words like 'dreadful news' and 'terrible news' were used by newscasters and presenters.

In a more general way, too, the language used in the mass media to describe ethnic minority and Third World issues both reflects the attitudes of those who work in them and sets the agenda for discussion. The words 'tribe' and 'tribalism' exemplify this. The media refers to every ethnic group in Africa as a 'tribe'. Yet each of these groups developed in a different way. There are 3 million Welsh and they are a nation, yet 3 million Baganda are a 'tribe'. Why aren't they (and the Zulu, and the Shona) described as 'nations' too? Similarly, in reporting disturbances in inner cities, the word 'riot' is often used whereas 'uprising', 'rebellion' or 'civil unrest' might be more accurate. Describing such disturbances as 'riots' neatly sidesteps any implications of deprivation that may have caused them and confirms the stereotype of blacks in conflict with the police.

● The numbers of black people seen on TV screens and in films are far less than their numbers in the population of Britain and (especially) the world. In the US about 97 per cent of all daytime serial characters are white and the rest mainly black. In prime-time serials the percentage is a little more realistic; 87 per cent are white. In comics and children's books black people are still largely absent, and when they do appear it is usually in one of the stereotyped roles discussed above.

● Where black people appear on the screens, they are portrayed in a patronising way, shown in a subordinate relationship to whites and in the wrong. This reflects the colonial and neo-colonial relationship between black and white countries internationally and perpetuates the myth of 'The White Man's Burden' (ie the duty to civilise the natives). Perhaps the most blatant example of this is the representation of American Indians in Western films. Portrayed as dangerous primitives, enemies of the peaceful whites, the reality was somewhat different. Similarly films like *Zulu* show no historical awareness of the nature of colonialism, merely characterising the 'natives' as unreasonably war-mongering and inadequate in the face of superior white civilization. *Band Aid's* song 'Do They Know It's Christmas?' reveals these sorts of attitudes. An African Muslim probably wouldn't want to know whether it's Christmas or not. Books such as the classic *Robinson Crusoe* are filled with these sorts of attitudes. Although this is an eighteenth century novel, it is still widely read and versions of it seen on film. Children's programmes like *Blue Peter* introduce such notions at an early age, as Bob Ferguson shows in his semiological reading of that programmes' account of a Pacific Island prince's visit to and subsequent death in Britain. (See the Bibliography at the end of this chapter for details.)

- Black people are low down in the hierarchy of access to the media, so that their point of view is rarely heard. They are 'invisible' in much the same way that women are. John Downing conducted a year-long study of 75 per cent of main TV output. During that time he found only forty-three items on discrimination in housing, employment, education, street attacks on blacks, black resistance and poor police-black relations. All of these are central issues to blacks, yet the first three, for example, received a total of eight minutes news time and forty-five minutes of current affairs time. More typical was the handling of a black march on Caledonian Road police station, sparked off by what was seen by the demonstrators as the unjust arrest of some black youths at a nearby fair and by concern for their safety in the police station. Rather than explaining this aspect of the story, *News at Ten* reported shouts of 'fascist pig', arrests of demonstrators, assaults on the police and damage of property by the demonstrators. The press reporting was in the same mould:

MOB RAID POLICE HQ—11 HURT

PC'S HURT IN LONDON BATTLE
(Both from *The Mirror*)

In other words the 'conflict' frame of reference discussed above was adopted.

- Black people are the butt of racist jokes in the press and on TV and radio. While often justified on the basis that they make whites laugh at their own prejudices, research by C. Husband finds that laughter confirms and reinforces racism. As we saw earlier (page 27) programmes like *In Sickness and in Health* will confirm the prejudices of those who already hold them, a finding supported by the BBC's own research, as Husband relates.

Examine the headlines and the editorials of the popular press over a one week period. Can you find similar examples of contradictory messages, particularly about race but also any other issues?

In fairness to the press, it should be pointed out that not all parts of it are guilty of the accusations levelled above. While *headlines* and news stories may be racist in tone, the *editorials*, even in the popular press, may be liberal and non- or even anti-racist.

Moreover some papers are more reasoned than others in their coverage of 'race' issues. *The Guardian*'s coverage of race issues, as

□ **BBC's soap opera *EastEnders* consciously tries to avoid racial stereotypes. How far do you think it is successful in this?**

revealed by Hartmann *et al*'s content analysis, has been 'thorough and wide-ranging'. In the broadcasting media too, efforts are often made to show racism being countered by reasoned argument and by punishment, while some programmes go out of their way to be non- or anti-racist.

To conclude this section, it is clear that, as with other areas of the representation of reality, the media's treatment of ethnic groups:

USES STEREOTYPICAL IMAGES OF BLACK PEOPLE

HAS A CLEAR INFERENTIAL STRUCTURE—RACE ISSUES ARE SIMPLIFIED AND GIVEN MEANINGS ACCORDING TO PARTICULAR NEWS VALUES

SETS THE AGENDA FOR THE DISCUSSION OF RACE ISSUES

HAS A HIERARCHY OF ACCESS WHICH LARGELY EXCLUDES BLACKS

□ **A number of pressure groups are concerned about the portrayal of ethnic minorities in the media. One is:**
The Campaign for Press and Broadcasting Freedom
9 Poland Street
London
WIV 3DG
Tel: 01 437 2795

Write to them or phone them and ask for a copy of their *Code of Conduct on Media Racism*. In class, discuss whether you agree with the code and how the aims it encompasses might best be achieved.

Another group you could contact for literature is:
The Campaign Against Racism in the Media (CARM)
BOX 50
London N1

The reasons for the biased treatment of ethnic groups

For *pluralists* the poor media representation of ethnic minorities in the past reflected the disadvantaged position of these groups in society. However, this has improved over the years as the media images of black people have started to become fairer and the stereotyped images used less often.

In support of this claim, pluralists can point to members of ethnic minorities in authoritative positions in British television. Well-known examples are presenters like Moira Stewart and Trevor MacDonald, but there are many others in both local and national media. Programmes for ethnic minorities such as *Black on Black*, *Ebony* etc. are increasingly given air time. Furthermore, there is an increasing amount of time given to black culture in general in the broadcast media, while in the publishing world there has been a rapid growth in recent years in the number of magazines catering especially for ethnic minorities as their presence and their spending power has come to be recognised. This view is confirmed by those at the top. Controller of BBC 1 Michael Grade said in an interview on *The Black and White Media Show* that:

There are more minority faces in positions of responsibility in the factual area as presenters, reporters, newscasters and so on, and that's a tremendous step forward.

(Though he did go on to say that there are still many problems in fictional programmes and comedy.)

☐ 1. **Do you agree that such individuals and programmes are a move towards a fairer representation of blacks on TV, or do you see them as a form of 'tokenism'; a mere nod in the direction of equality?**

☐ 2. **There is considerable debate over TV programming for black people. Some argue that programmes for black people and about black issues are essential because of the inferior treatment they receive in mainstream broadcasting. Others argue that making such *separate* programmes is a form of televisual apartheid and tokenism. The answer is to involve black issues and black presenters in normal programming. Where do you stand in this debate?**

As far as the British *press* are concerned, the pluralist would say that they cannot be expected to analyse the underlying socio-economic causes of the problems ethnic minorities have. Their role is the day to day reporting of events as they occur. News values call for reporting of conflict. Readers would quickly switch allegiance if *The Sun* or *The Star* had long and detailed analyses of discriminatory practices in employment and housing. Media reporting of race, as with other issues, is in-line with what the public want. This is identified by news editors, revealed by newspaper sales and disclosed by public opinion research.

With reference to the *American* mass media, particularly film, one American writer in the pluralist mould argues that:

While the real world has made faltering progress toward integrating the negro in the mainstream of American life, the fantasy world—that exhibited primarily by the mass media— is portraying him as a fully-fledged member of society. This represents a significant change in the Negro image in the mass media, for where once only white cowboys rode the range, now spurs, six shooters and ten-gallon hats adorn negroes as well. In place of servant, dance and 'crap-shooting' roles, negroes are seen throughout the US and much of the rest of the world as espionage agents, psychologists, judges, nurses and just plain people.

The change is attributable to the following factors:

● key organisations in the mass media espoused a non-discriminatory policy from the mid-1960s onwards

● positive action (demo's etc) became more forceful

● minority groups became stronger and more articulate

● legal action was taken where employment policies etc did not conform to new, liberal, laws

● marketing conditions changed so that films were being sold abroad to countries which wanted black people seen on the screen in important roles

□ **Is it true that in Britain, too, black people are getting a fairer showing in the media?**

What examples can you give to demonstrate that it is (or it isn't).

If there has been an improvement in the situation in Britain, are the reasons for this the same as they were in the United States?

- industry training programmes began to provide talented black actors, writers and so on

- independent producers became more important as the power of the monolithic picture houses such as Paramount began to decline. These producers were much more willing to use black actors in realistic roles

- pioneering black actors such as Sidney Poitier served as examples for others to follow

- the social climate changed so that racial discrimination and overtly stereotyped presentations of blacks became unacceptable

The same viewpoint, but related to American advertisements, is found in an article in *New Society* (summer 1987). The argument is that in the US black people are portrayed in positive roles in advertisements, but this was not the case in the past. The change is due to the affluence of the black market now and to political strength, exemplified by the success of the campaign by Jesse Jackson to get Coca Cola to change its advertising and employment practices. He asked black people to drink Pepsi instead until Coke did so; it soon did! In Britain, though, the old racial stereotypes still linger in some advertising because of the lack of black political power and limited spending power black people have.

In *The Mass Media and Racial Conflict* Paul Hartmann and Charles Husband suggest two main reasons for the biased representation of ethnic minorities in the British media, the press in particular:

1. That portraying black people as a "problem" coincides with journalists' ideas about what is newsworthy, ie their news values. Fear, tension, conflict etc are words which make the audience sit up and take notice. Coexistence, harmony, and peace are words which just don't get into the news. One possible exception is the Notting Hill carnival with the obligatory picture of the smiling policeman joining in, though even this has a frisson provided by the ever-present threat of trouble, a fear confirmed in the 1987 carnival.

2. That in providing these images of black people in the media, journalists and others responsible for them are merely reflecting back to society the derogatory attitudes and negative symbols concerning foreigners and blacks which are inherent in the British culture.

Hartmann and Husband therefore partly subscribe to the pluralist model of the media; the media don't shape society, they are shaped by it. As whites brought up in Western society we have racism stamped on our consciousness. Our assumptions, judgements and feelings are permeated with attitudes inherited from centuries of colonialism and racism, and are hence untrustworthy.

Marxists and neo-Marxists in particular are very dismissive of this approach. Marxists feel that these authors have not really addressed why the ideology of racism persists, or why news values are as they are. A more radical approach sees the reasons for the unique treatment of black people as based in the nature of British capitalism.

This says it is in the interests of British capitalism to set white worker against black (who can be easily scapegoated because of their skin colour) for a number of reasons:

- black workers are blamed for unemployment (too many blacks taking jobs, not by the inevitable crises in capitalist production)

- unions will not defend black workers and so low wages and poor conditions prevail where black workers predominate. They can be 'super-exploited' by the capitalist class

- workers will be disunited and, therefore, not put forward an effective opposition to capitalism

- white workers will feel relatively privileged compared to blacks and their militancy will be correspondingly reduced.

☐ **Would you agree or disagree with this perspective? What evidence or argument can you bring to bear to support your point of view?**

This perspective can be found in books such as *The Empire Strikes Back* and *Immigrant Workers and Class Structure in Western Europe*.

In them it is suggested that the role of the media is to shape the views of white workers, encouraging them to blame black immigrants for problems which are really the inevitable consequences of the capitalist system. These include unemployment, low wages, lack of decent housing, inner city deprivation, violence on the streets, and poor schooling ('they're taking our jobs/homes', 'they're turning inner cities into no-go areas', 'schools can't teach in English any more', etc). In this way, those who suffer most from bad conditions are blamed for them. Such *fractionalisation* of the working class is clearly in the interests of the capitalist class, and the media are their tool in this.

Most Marxists, and many others, would argue that racism in the media is not the result of a *deliberate* attempt to manipulate attitudes. Rather, those who hold powerful positions and can decide what does and does not get into the media have racist attitudes themselves, often more so than the population at large because of their particular social background and training. This is a version of the hegemonic perspective (see page 37). One of the ways this hegemony is reinforced is through the selective employment practices that go on in the media. There are very few representatives of ethnic minorities working in the media, particularly not in the more senior positions. Thus, the 'black' perspective on issues is rarely voiced. One exception, Juliet Alexander, who was once a reporter on the Hackney Gazette in East London, tells how in her initial interview for the job her editor told her that he was 'killing two minorities in one'. Alex Pacall relates the difficulties he had as one of the few blacks working for Radio London in the 1970s and '80s. His programme *Black Londoners* caused particular difficulties with the BBC management. He writes:

> *The programme was in fact intended for the White liberal element who sponsor what passes for black culture, black programmes made for White people from a White point of view, as part of the contribution to the anti-racist struggle.*
>
> *Hence they expect us to be in a state of high exultation, and gracefully receive the crumbs from the Master's table.*

The prejudiced views of editors are illustrated in the following account the handling of a story by a London radio station. A black journalist on the station gained an interview with the black victim of unlawful arrest and malicious wounding by the Metropolitan Police. He had suffered a broken leg in the back of a police van and was awarded damages by the High Court for this and the arrest. The journalist wrote the story along the lines of 'aggrieved man wins victory over bullying cops'. But the editor changed it so that the bulletin eventually reported how the man's neighbours thought he was a bit mad because he wore African clothes in the winter. There was very little background about the events or the case. The editor's explanation was that he was making a heavy story lighter so it would be more acceptable to a wider audience. This racist approach resulted from his ideas about black people as colourful characters not to be taken seriously and from his concept of 'news values'.

In television the same sort of thing occurs. In fiction programmes there are very few black actors. *It Ain't Half Hot, Mum* used white actors to play Indians. Tony Freeth, a freelance producer, was told by someone in the BBC that 'the leading actor [in that series] loves Indians, in fact he thinks the British should never have left India'. It is not suprising that few black people are seen in TV advertisements when we learn from a senior executive of Saatchi and Saatchi that only one copywriter out of its 800-odd employees is black.

The authors of *Policing the Crisis* subscribe to a neo-Marxist explanation of media racism, though they are perhaps more radical than many in their interpretation of it. They consider that the *primary definers* of what is 'important news' and what the 'correct' perspective on that news should be are the politicians, police and business leaders. The ideas of such people have hegemony in society and in the media, the latter because their ideas become integrated into concepts of *news values*, *professional journalism* and so on. For example, once race relations in Britain have become defined by these primary definers as 'a problem of numbers', this is picked up by the media. Other viewpoints (such as the multiple disadvantages suffered by ethnic minorities) do not see the light of day and even liberal spokesmen and women are forced to conduct the debate on this ground.

Thus, the problem lies not only *within* media institutions, according to this view, but also with the sources used by them. Crime reporters lean heavily on 'official sources' such as Scotland Yard and the police in general for their crime reporting. Checking it against other sources or looking for other angles on a story would undermine the hotline to a valuable source of news. Thus, journalists are fed the official, white and police version of events. One effect of this is that the socio-political causes of events such as the "riots" in Brixton in 1981, and others like them, are ignored. The 'criminal angle' is the one that gets the attention in the news. This cosy relationship between the police PR departments and the media is evident in stories like the marriage between an Asian PC and a white policewoman (a splash story in both *The Express* and *The Mirror*) and a TV news item showing black sixth formers visiting New Scotland Yard.

All this is not to deny that the media on occasion may *deliberately* manipulate the presentation of race issues. B. Parekh, Professor of Political Theory at Hull University, recounts how the press distorted two stories (one about Brent's appointment of 177 staff to deal with the underachievement of ethnic minority children and the other about a change in the visa requirements for Commonwealth countries). Parekh concludes that '. . . the press twists facts, tells lies, declares a cold war on a section of the community, uses editorials as party political broadcasts and subjects its readers to a daily breakfast of raw prejudices . . .'

☐ **Examine as many sources of news as possible in one day. Identify those items which appear to emanate from police PR departments or similar sources (for example companies, universities etc).**

The reasons for the lies and twisting of the truth are not explored by Parekh, but it is clear that he believes that there is a very deliberate attempt to manipulate people's attitudes towards ethnic minorities in Britain.

3. The effects of the biased treatment of ethnic groups

People's attitudes undergo fairly major changes as a result of exposure to media reporting of race issues. Hartmann *et al* in a UNESCO study (1974) conducted a survey to find out whether there was any correspondence between media content and people's views of race relations. They discovered that there was such a correspondence. Many of their respondents claimed to have obtained most of their ideas about race from the media.

A study by Hartmann and Husband on the attitudes towards race of children aged 11–12 and 14–15 years yielded similar results. Part of the sample selected for study lived in the West Midlands and Yorkshire (where there is a high density of coloured people) and a second part lived in Teeside and Glasgow (where there is not). Hartmann and Husband found that children in the latter areas were more likely to view race relations in terms of 'conflict', 'threat' and 'numbers' because they were gaining virtually all of their information on the issue from the media rather than from actual experience.

It is no surprise to learn from the British Social Attitudes Survey of 1984, therefore, that:

- 91 per cent of people think Britain is a racially prejudiced country

- 33 per cent of people are prepared to state openly that they are prejudiced against black people

- 40 per cent think that racial tensions will worsen in Britain in the future.

There are important political effects when people's attitudes are shaped by the media rather than reflecting them. If people are led like sheep along certain lines of thought then their political power, their ability to shape events is destroyed. Rather than political power residing with the people, it rests with those who, through the mass media, shape the attitudes of the people.

In the short term people's attitudes to particular events can be moulded, especially where there is a deliberate campaign to do this in the press. Politicians occasionally use the media to stir up public feeling (Enoch Powell did this on the immigration issue in the late 1960s). Pressure groups do much the same thing. An example is the case of Bradford headmaster, Ray Honeyford, who was suspended and eventually removed from his post for apparently racist remarks in a right wing journal. He was defended by his professional association and much of the media treatment of the case was very sympathetic towards him. A similar issue arose in 1987 when parents in Dewsbury withdrew their children from a school in which the pupils were predominantly Asian. This was a situation given very heavy treatment by both broadcast and published media, despite the small number of parents involved.

☐ 1. What race issues are in the media at the moment or have been recently?

2. Was the media reporting fair and unbiased in your view?

3. What may have been the effect of the media reporting of these issues?

If the media reinforce and feed racial *prejudice* (pre-conceived negative views about coloured people), this will soon be translated into racial *discrimination* (acting in a different way towards people on the basis of their skin colour). Thus, the media are at least partly to blame for the disadvantages suffered by coloured people in Britain in terms of:

access to jobs
promotion opportunities
access to good housing
access to a good standard of education

and other inequalities such as those documented in studies conducted by the Policy Studies Institute in 1984 and 1985.

In the same way, racially motivated attacks on blacks will be at least partly inspired by their stereotypical presentation in the media and the scapegoat function they perform. A Home Office study published in 1981 showed that Asians were fifty times more likely to be the victims of racial attacks than whites. The figure for West Indians was thirty-six times.

The working class are divided and blacks are left unsupported by largely white institutions such as unions partly as a result of the racism which the media propagate. This lack of integration of black workers into white institutions has been documented by, for example, Rex and Tomlinson in their study of Handsworth.

As we saw earlier (page 67), the effect of moral panics in the media about black immigration and criminality (particularly 'mugging') is, according to the authors of *Policing the Crisis*, to influence public opinion so that the capitalist state can be strengthened by the implementation of 'firm steps'. These may take the form of legislation restricting civil rights, criminalising certain forms of activity or increasing levels of punishment. Police powers and resources are often increased in the wake of this sort of moral panic. The overall aim is to gain a consensus in favour of a tightening of control over the population as a whole so that the inherently unstable capitalist system can be held together, by the use of force and repression if necessary.

As a result of '*The coup–war–famine syndrome*', the view is propagated that Third World underdevelopment, poverty and backwardness is due to black stupidity, barbarism, laziness, corruption, unstable political regimes and/or climatic disaster. More sophisticated views, such as the idea that the Third World's poverty may be due to its dependency relationship with the West, are ignored.

In conclusion, it should be said that the media are not the only social institutions which influence attitudes towards coloured minorities. People learn attitudes on these issues from other sources too. Even people who live in areas where they rarely meet a coloured person will unconsciously pick up attitudes from elsewhere. The English language which tends to associate black with bad (accident black spot, black sheep, etc) is the source of many of these.

☐ **List other words or phrases in the English language which are anti-black.**

Early socialisation will also transmit values which have their roots in the colonial past; ideas about 'savages', cannibalism and the rest. The media, then, do not only influence attitudes, they also reflect them. We bring to the media a 'perceptual set'; a set of expectations about what we see and what it means. Much of this is gained elsewhere. How we interpret media messages will largely depend on the nature of this perceptual set.

☐ The following two exercises illustrate the notion of the perceptual set.

1.

How does this diagram illustrate the notion of 'perceptual set'?

2. The following are actual newspaper headlines. If you are working in a group, write a short summary of the story you think followed them individually, then compare your stories to see how closely your version matches that of the other members of the group:

GET THEM OFF OUR STREETS

THEY SHALL NOT WIN

FLAMES OF HATE

(*The Star*, *Express* and *The Star* respectively)

☐ **PROJECT**

This project uses content-analysis to establish the degree of exposure given to ethnic minorities on TV and to compare different channels on this.

Prepare a time sample sheet which you will be able to tick as you watch broadcast TV, recording the time devoted to representatives of ethnic minorities and details of their portrayal. The following gives some very basic ideas for you to develop:

☐ **ESSAY**

What evidence is there of the use of racial stereotypes in the mass media and to what extent do such stereotypes influence social attitudes towards ethnic minorities?

Occasions	Minutes exposure	Main or subsidiary character	Positive or negative portrayal	Programme type	ETC
1					
2					
3 etc					

On successive nights watch the output of just one channel for a pre-determined amount of time, filling in the sheets as you do so and supplementing this with notes where necessary. You will need a stop-watch to time each occasion on which a black person appears.

Having done this for all four channels, collate and write up your material, including an assessment of the method used and suggestions for improvement as well as an analysis of the results.

Bibliography

C. Brown, *Black and White Britain: the Third PSI Survey*, Heinemann, London, 1984

C. Brown and P. Gay, *Racial Discrimination: Seventeen Years After the Act*, PSI, London, 1985

J. Rex and S. Tomlinson, *Colonial Immigrants in a British City*, Routledge and Kegan Paul, London 1979

Centre for Contemporary Cultural Studies, *The Empire Strikes Back*, Hutchinson, London, 1982

S. Castles and G. Kosack, *Immigrant Workers and Class Structure in Western Europe*, Oxford University Press, Oxford, 1973

S. Hall, *et al*, *Policing the Crisis: Mugging, the State and Law and Order*, Macmillan, London, 1978

C. Husband, *The Mass Media and the Function of Humour in a Racist Society* in A. J. Chapman and H.C. Frost, (eds), *It's a Funny Thing, Humour*, Pergamon Press, Oxford, 1977

R.F. Hixon (ed), *Mass Media: A Casebook*, Thomas Y. Crowell, New York, 1973, see especially R.D. Colle, *Negro Image in the Mass Media: A Case Study in Social Change*, pp. 71–80. This is the source of the material about the improved American media treatment of black people.

R. Harris, *Gotcha!*, Faber and Faber, London, 1983

Glasgow University Media Group, *War and Peace News*, Open University Press, Milton Keynes, 1985

B. Parekh, *Prejudice and the Press*, New Society, 7 November 1986. This is the source of the quote page 120

J. Twitchin, (ed), *The Black and White Media Book*, Trentham Books, Stoke-on-Trent, forthcoming

J. Downing, *The Media Machine*, Pluto Press, London, 1980.

P. Cohen and C. Gardner, *It Ain't Half Racist Mum*, Comedia, London, 1985. This is the source of the quotes from Juliet Alexander and Alex Pacall (both page 9)

D. Lipsey, *A Black Mark For Advertisers*, New Society, 21 August 1987, pages 11–13. This is the source of the commentary about black people in advertising in Britain and America.

R. Smith, *Black Journalists and the White Media* in *Race and Society*. New Society, 2 October 1987, pages 6–8. This is the source of the story about the black man who won damages from the Metropolitan Police

O. Boyd-Barrett and P. Braham, *Media. Knowledge and Power*, Croom Helm, 1987

M. Alvarado, R. Gutch and P. Wollen, *Learning the Med.* Macmillan, 1987

B. Ferguson, *Black Blue Peter*, in L. Masterman, (ed), *Television Mythologies*, Comedia, London, 1986

J. Fiske and J. Hartley, *Reading Television*, Methuen, London, 1978, see especially pages 174–7

J. Hartley, *et al*, *Making Sense of the Media*, Comedia, London, 1985, see especially Block 1, Unit 2.

C. Husband, *White Media and Black Britain*, Arrow Books, London, 1975

J. D. Halloran, (ed), *Race as News*, UNESCO Press, Paris, 1974, see especially P. Hartmann, *et al*, *Race as News: a study in the handling of race in the British National Press for 1963–1970*. This is the source of the table

C. Seymour-Ure, *The Political Impact of the Mass Media*, Constable, London, 1974

M. Cantor and S. Pingree, *The Soap Opera*, Sage, 1983. Figures for the percentage of blacks in soap opera quoted in the text come from this book quoting B.S. Greenberg, *et al*, *What's on the Soaps and Who Cares?*, Journal of Broadcasting 26: 519–36 (daytime serials) and N. Signorelli, *The Demography of the TV World*, paper presented to a US symposium on the media in February 1982 (prime-time serials)

J. Downing, *The (balanced) White View*, in C. Husband, *op cit* 1975

P. Golding. *The Mass Media*, Longman, London, 1974, the quote is from page 84

Videos

It Ain't Half Racist, Mum, (an Open Door film), available from Concord Films, 201 Felixstowe Road, Ipswich, Suffolk.

Black and White Media Shows (two programmes) available from the NUT, Hamilton House, Mabledon Place, London WC1 9BD or from their producer, John Twitchin, Villiers House, Ealing Broadway, London W5 2PA

General Bibliography

D. Glover, *Sociology of the Mass Media*, Causeway Press, 1984

B. Dutton, *The Media*, Longman, London, 1986

D. Barrat, *Media Sociology*, Tavistock, London, 1986

J. Hartley, *et al*, *Making Sense of the Media*, Comedia, London, 1985

J. Tunstall, *The Media in Britain*, Constable, London, 1983

J. Curran, *et al*, *Bending Reality*, Pluto, London, 1986

P. Golding, *The Mass Media*, 6th edition, Longman, London, 1984

A. Hetherington, *News, Newspapers and Television*, Macmillan, London, 1985

J. Fiske, *Introduction to Communication Studies*, Comedia, London, 1982

T. O'Sullivan, *et al*, *Key Concepts in Communication*, Comedia, London, 1983

Subject Index

Author Index

Acknowledgements

The author and publisher are indebted to the following:

For permission to reproduce text extracts:

Basil Blackwell for material from *The Language of Advertising* by T Vestergaard and K Schroeder; BBC Enterprises Ltd for material reproduced from *EastEnders: The Inside Story* by Julia Smith and Tony Holland; Grafton Books, a division of the Collins Publishing Group, for material from *What a Man's Gotta Do* by A Easthope; Gowar Publishing Group for material from *Forever Feminine* by M Ferguson; The Controller of HMSO for two tables from *Social Trends 17*, 1987; The IBA for two tables from *Attitudes to Broadcasting*, two tables from the *IBA Yearbook 1987* and an extract from the *IBA Annual Report and Accounts 1984–5*; Macmillan Publishers Ltd for material from *News, Newspapers and TV* by A Hetherington; Marion Boyars for material from *Decoding Advertisements* by J Williamson and *Consuming Passions* by J Williamson; *News on Sunday* for their *Editorial Charter*; Routledge & Kegan Paul for material from *Feminism for Girls* by A McRobbie and I McCabe; The University of Queensland Press for material from *Children and Screen Violence* by P Edgar.

While every effort has been made to contact copyright-holders, this has not proved possible in every case. The publishers would be pleased to hear from any copyright-holders not acknowledged.

For permission to reproduce illustrations:

BBC Enterprises Ltd, pp 27, 48, 82, 95, 101, 111
Camden Press Ltd, p 40
Camera Press Ltd, p 34
Channel 4 Television, p 97
Comedia Publishing Group, p 83
The Daily Telegraph, p 88
EMI Ltd, p 54
Express Newspapers, p 88
The Guardian, p 88
The Independent, p 88

Johnson and Johnson, p 80
Lisa Ash, p 19
Mac, p 110
Mail Newspapers, pp 88, 110
Popperfoto, p 50
Rediffusion, pp 5, 8, 9
The Sun, p 88
Steve Bell, pp 30, 69
Syndication International, p 88
Times Newspapers Ltd 1987, p 88